Super Healthy Snacks and Treats

Super Healthy Snacks and Treats

More than 60 easy recipes for
energizing, delicious snacks free from
gluten, dairy, refined sugar and eggs

JENNA ZOE

Photography by Clare Winfield

RYLAND PETERS & SMALL
LONDON • NEW YORK

Dedication

To Mama Jaan, who always cooked
with loving intentions

Senior designer Lucy Gowans
Commissioning editor Céline Hughes
Production manager Gordana Simakovic
Art director Leslie Harrington
Editorial director Julia Charles

Food stylist Jenna Zoe
Food styling assistants
  Kathy Kordalis
  Emily Kydd
  Rosie Reynolds
Prop stylist Polly Webb-Wilson
Indexer Sandra Shotter

First published in 2013 by
Ryland Peters & Small
20–21 Jockey's Fields
London WC1R 4BW
and
519 Broadway, 5th Floor
New York, NY 10012
www.rylandpeters.com

10 9 8 7 6 5 4 3 2 1

Text © Jenna Zoe 2013
Design and photographs
© Ryland Peters & Small 2013

Printed in China

ISBN: 978-1-84975-428-6

A CIP record for this book is available from the British
Library.

US Library of Congress Cataloging-in-Publication data
has been applied for.

Neither the author nor the publisher can be held
responsible for any claim arising out of the information
in this book. Always consult your health advisor or
doctor if you have any concerns about your health
or nutrition.

Notes
• If you are allergic to gluten, wheat, sugar, dairy, eggs
or soy, please check all labelling carefully before buying
ingredients for use in these recipes.
• Oats are inherently gluten free, but because they are
mostly processed in facilities that also process glutenous
grains, most brands are cross-contaminated with gluten
and therefore not suitable for coeliacs. If you need to
avoid gluten entirely, look for oats that are labelled
"gluten-free".
• All spoon measurements are level unless otherwise
specified.
• Ovens should be preheated to the specified
temperature. Recipes in this book were tested using
a regular oven. If using a fan-assisted oven, follow the
manufacturer's instructions for adjusting temperatures.
• When a recipe calls for the grated zest of citrus fruit,
buy unwaxed fruit and wash well before use. If you can
only find treated fruit, scrub well in warm soapy water
and rinse before using.
• Find all the healthy ingredients and baking staples
mentioned in this book on its accompanying website,
www.foodstolove.co.uk
• Here are some of my favourite healthy living blogs:
www.foodbabe.com
www.hungryhungryhippie.com
www.fitnessista.com
www.katheats.com
thinkoutsidethecerealbox.tumblr.com
www.calgaryavansino.com
www.kimberlysnyder.net/blog
www.detoxinista.com

YouTube Channels:
FullyRaw Kristina
DaraDubinet

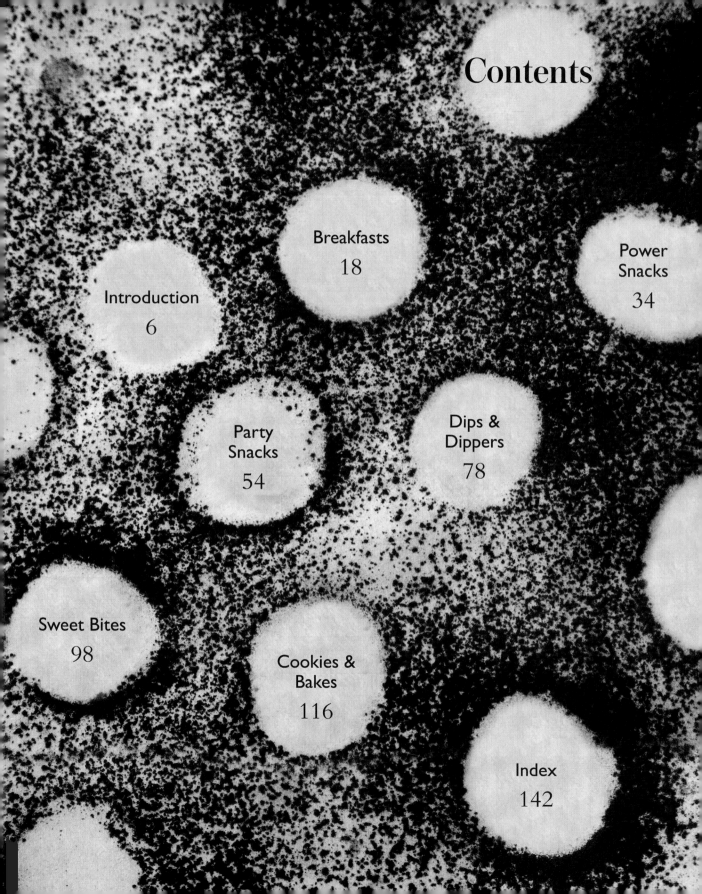

Contents

Adjusting our attitude to food

In terms of food and nutrition, we are living in a funny time – on the one hand, we have never had more great products available to us, never had more information about nutrients and the ways in which they work. While more knowledge is always a good thing, this can also be a recipe for information overload and "decision fatigue". We have never been so confused as to what to eat and how to eat it. It's ironic that so many of us feel so much anxiety and inadequacy around an act so seemingly simple, something mandatory for our survival.

The truth is, there are infinite ways to be healthy, and infinite combinations of meals that we can eat in order to get there – it's overwhelming. We want to believe there's one ready-made solution out there that will fit us perfectly. I certainly did. To that end, I've been through almost every eating style around. I've cut out carbs, eaten like a caveman, done macrobiotics, five small meals a day, no sugar, food combining – you name it. I may have felt healthy enough in any given phase, but I always knew with every bone in my body that I could feel better. I envisaged feeling happy and vibrant and full of energy while eating in a way that felt effortless, joyous and intuitive, as opposed to carefully controlled and filled with anxiety about failing.

When this cycle of feeling dissatisfied with other people's rules continued, I decided to change my tactic; I said to myself, there is a perfect diet out there for me, but it's my job to design it. Immediately, things felt different. I felt empowered. Things started to look up as I promised myself that going forward, I would do things my way. I didn't know what that meant yet, but the foods I was going to eat had to fulfil three criteria:
• They had to be natural, whole foods that were minimally processed (most of the time).
• I had to LOVE how they tasted. I didn't force myself to eat anything I didn't like, even if it was meant to be good for me. I was game to taste anything once, but after that there was no obligation to continue.
• They had to suit my system. I paid close attention to what made me bloated or sluggish, what I didn't digest well, and in what combinations certain things disagreed with me.

Of course, I didn't have it all figured out right out of the gate. It took trial and error, but I didn't consider it failure – it was one big (and exciting) experiment.

As I became more in tune with how certain foods acted in my body, I realized that I felt better when I didn't eat things like gluten, wheat, dairy, eggs, soy, and refined sugars. These are common allergens that cause discomfort among many people, and while I wasn't intolerant to any of them, they made me feel just "OK" rather than amazing.

I asked myself, why should anyone settle for anything less than amazing? Nowadays, this is the approach that I recommend to my clients. Reclaim the power over your health and body. Chase "amazing" because we all deserve it. In fact, the human body is designed for amazing, and it's more than capable of getting there on its own. The only thing we have to do is give it the tools (proper fuel) to do its job.

With the dishes in this book, you will be giving your body all good things. They will take you from everyday snacks to special-occasion treats while always remaining on the healthful side of the spectrum. This isn't your typical earthy, rustic healthy food – it's food full of fun and colour because I refuse to believe those are things we should have to sacrifice when we choose to treat our bodies well. I like to infuse my daily eats with brightness and positivity, because mental health is a big part of our overall wellbeing too.

I hope that the recipes in this book can inspire you to make your own healthy eating rules, and help you feel empowered to take the best care of your most precious asset – YOU!

The principles of healthy snacking

Every time we eat, we can either choose to eat foods that help our bodies thrive, or hinder it on its course. Sticking to clean, simple foods that nature made not only helps us look better, but is also the key to that happy, energetic, thriving state that seems so elusive to so many of us.

Around 30% of our bodies' energy is used in the digestion process. When we consume overly processed foods that our bodies don't recognize, a lot more energy is allocated to digesting these and flushing out their toxins. Think of it as a drain on our bodies' resources, because this energy could be better used for thousands of other functions the body needs to perform. Poor digestion is a significant contributor to low energy levels, sluggishness, poor mood control, slow healing or recovery, and premature ageing, because digestion is using up the energy that should be going towards these things.

There are more "healthy" convenience foods available to us than ever, but it's become more difficult to figure out how healthful they truly are. Widely acknowledged nasties such as white sugar, MSG and trans fats lurk everywhere as their healthier-sounding alter egos. To add to that, allergies and intolerances to components like wheat, gluten, dairy, sugar and eggs are reaching epidemic proportions.

The benefits of avoiding wheat, gluten, dairy, sugar and eggs

How allergies and intolerances work

An allergy is a reaction by the immune system to a foreign substance it considers an enemy. Often, allergies are embedded in our DNA and so cannot be reversed. If you have an allergy, it means that a food doesn't suit your entire system, which is why our skin and blood will react to this food too. Allergies are often immediate and measurable.

An intolerance, on the other hand, is localized to our digestive system, ie the stomach has difficulty breaking down a certain substance. This often occurs when we overconsume a food, because we exhaust the tools our bodies use to break down said food. Symptoms of an intolerance can be subtle and difficult to trace back to the original culprit.

Whereas we have been familiar with the concept of allergies for years, the epidemic levels of food intolerances has only been a recent phenomenon. This is because the modern diet is not varied enough and heavily features the mass-produced, subsidized commodities that we are now having trouble eating. Whether or not you have an intolerance, it's a good idea to try to rely less on these common foods, and focus on a variety of fruit and vegetables as the base of your diet.

Cutting them out

The key to making substitutions for allergens in your diet is that it doesn't need to be all-or-nothing. For most people, being rigid about what you can and can't have doesn't work. Even if you have the strongest willpower and the best intentions, life happens – we travel, get stuck, run late, get busy, don't hear the alarm clock, and sometimes we just plain old can't-be-bothered. I tell everybody that if you *plan* to eat well for the times in your week where you *can* eat well, it doesn't matter about the few times when you give yourself a little more leeway. Whether that's because you simply don't have access to the healthier options, or because you decide that you want to indulge in your favourite meal tonight, it doesn't matter. The overall picture of your diet is what will predict your wellbeing.

As soon as you start to eat a little more "cleanly" than before, you will feel and look better, no matter where your starting point lies. This new way of eating will soon become your

THE PRINCIPLES OF HEALTHY SNACKING 9

norm; stay in that zone until it feels easy and natural to you, and at some point you will feel inspired to take it to the next level. Don't rush yourself or force yourself to clean up too fast – your body has an innate wisdom regarding what it's ready for.

Wheat and gluten

"Gluten-free" is a huge selling point for food producers nowadays, but ask anyone to tell you what gluten is and why it's best avoided, and you're unlikely to get an answer. I've even come across people who work in this industry and can't explain it – this is primarily because it's a complex issue without one clear root "problem". Gluten is a protein found in most grains, and it is the type of gluten found in wheat, barley and rye that mostly cause intolerance (these are wheat gluten, hordein and secalin respectively).

The heightened gluten levels in our diet are down to two primary factors. Firstly, we overconsume it without even trying. Gluten is added to an unbelievable variety of common pantry products because it performs plenty of helpful functions. It is what gives bread its soft, doughy texture, so food producers used it to increase the mouthfeel of their goods, such as bottled sauces and ready-made baked products. It also acts as a preservative and can be used to increase shelf life. Extracting gluten and adding it to a food is relatively cheap and easy to do, so it's a common solution.

Secondly, modern wheat has been genetically transformed in order to increase its yield per acre. Gliadin, the component in wheat gluten that causes intolerance, has been re-engineered to make this possible, and has morphed into a much more aggravating hybrid than that found in wheat in the 1950s.

Dairy products

If you asked me which single change could make the most significant improvement to your health, removing dairy products would be it. A mammal's milk is designed to help its infant increase in weight by up to eight times. It contains all the necessary goodness to help that calf, kid or foal grow. Once it has completed its growth, it stops drinking this milk.

Where it is the ideal fuel for a baby mammal, dairy milk is not designed for human consumption. Think about it, we are the only species on earth that consume the milk of another animal – and continue to do so past our main period of growth! Dairy products are very mucus-forming in the human body, causing all sorts of problems like excess phlegm, weight gain and inflammation.

Additionally, ask anyone you know why they think milk is good for them and they're highly likely to tell you something about how you need the calcium in it for your bone health. Dairy products do contain calcium, and it makes sense to assume that consuming milk, yogurt, cheese and the like would increase your body's calcium levels. However, this is only part of the picture. The body likes to maintain an internal environment with a slightly alkaline pH (the opposite being an acidic pH). This is the condition that allows it to function at its optimum level. An internal alkaline environment allows the necessary chemical processes to take place, whereas acidity is conducive to illness, fatigue, and free-radical formation. When faced with factors such as stress, pollution, inadequate rest and poor diet (all of which are acid-forming), the body will draw from its stores of alkaline minerals to counteract the effects of these factors on bodily pH.

The alkaline minerals in the body are calcium, magnesium, sodium and potassium, the most abundant of which is calcium, stored in the bones. Essentially, alkaline foods are those that contribute to your levels of these minerals, and acidic foods are the ones that deplete them.

Dairy is not a preferred source of energy for the body as it is difficult to digest and encourages the production of mucus. It is thus a source of digestive stress which in turn is acid-forming. In order to neutralize the acidic nature of this process, the body pulls calcium into the bloodstream from its bones. So, even though dairy brings some calcium into your system, there is a net loss of calcium when consuming it.

What's interesting is that in countries where the indigenous people consume little or no dairy, the instances of osteoporosis are extremely low. In Japan for example, where the traditional diet consists mainly of fish, vegetables, sea vegetables, soy and grains, the disease is practically unheard of. In almost every non-Caucasian country, the number of osteoporosis cases has risen in direct correlation with the adoption of Western dietary habits over the last few decades.

We have been told that we need milk for its calcium content, to the point where we have forgotten about all the plant-based sources of this nutrient – broccoli, collard greens, soy beans, sesame seeds, almonds, hemp seeds, figs, dates and apricots are all great options.

Eggs

You may be surprised to see eggs in this list because they are supposedly full of health benefits – high in protein, a rare source of choline, Vitamin D and lutein. However, just because something is good for us in some ways, it doesn't mean that it isn't also bad for us in other ways. Farming practices that surround raising chickens for eggs are so questionable, that even if you're an omnivore it's best to keep organic, cage-free eggs as an occasional food in your diet.

Eggs were not designed for humans to eat, and because our society is consuming them more than ever before, egg allergies are increasing to the point where they are now the second most common food allergen, behind milk. Adverse reactions are particularly high among children whose "purer" digestive systems find them hard to tolerate.

If you never want to go without eggs because you love the taste, which is totally understandable, I think it's best to reserve them for dishes where you can really taste them, and keep them out of your treats, where we can put plenty of other fun things in their place.

Eggs are the most difficult thing to replace in baking because they perform three separate functions, so sometimes we need to substitute them with more than two or three different ingredients which perform these various roles – providing texture, helping the mixture to rise, and acting as a binding agent.

Sugar

The health hazards of sugar are well known. High consumption of sugar has been shown to correlate with the big killers, ie heart disease, diabetes, heart attacks and cancer. While these are not necessarily factors I think about every day, I avoid white sugar because it throws our bodies off course; where the body likes to have even blood sugar, control of its moods and steady energy levels, sugar interrupts this preferred happy state. Ingesting refined sugars places such a heavy burden on the body that it has to work extra hard to stay happy.

Having said that, it's unrealistic to expect we will never again have a sweet treat. Luckily, there are amazing alternatives available to us nowadays that are much gentler on our bodies. The options on page 17 enables me to enjoy my sweet treats without feeling guilty about eating them at the same time. The importance of this cannot be underestimated; I truly believe that any negative emotions we ingest while eating, no matter how healthy the food is, manifest themselves in undesirable ways – be that weight gain, digestive upset, lack of satiation, or worse, that mental cycle of always feeling like food is our enemy.

How to use this book

A mistake I often used to make when I was first getting into using cookbooks was not reading the entire recipe through before starting to cook it. It seems obvious, but it's a must: not only does it give you an idea of the proper time frame and process required, but more crucially it helps us envisage how we're going to do something before attempting it. The cooking or baking itself will feel smoother and less chaotic if you take five quiet minutes to understand the recipe first.

Gather your ingredients, measuring tools and bowls before you do anything else. Having to source unusual ingredients often gets in the way of my being adventurous in the kitchen, so I created a website where you can find everything you'll need in one place and get it all delivered right to your door. Visit www.foodstolove.co.uk for all my favourite products used in this book.

Looking for suggestions on which recipe to try first? These are straightforward and the most undeniably delicious – the ones you're likely to make again and again:

All the recipes in the Dips & Dippers and Power Snacks chapters are also super easy to make.

Some of the recipes are more complex to prepare. I hesitate to use the word "difficult" because it's not that the recipes are tough; you just have to find your groove a little when you try them for the first time. I've often found that if I try to make a simpler cake right before making a more advanced one, the latter is more likely to turn out great. The secret ingredient? You've found your confidence in the kitchen already.

Gotta-get-in-your-groove recipes

Essential ingredients and substitutions

Xanthan gum

Xanthan gum is a natural gum that acts as a gluten substitute. The reason glutenous flours are so much easier to bake with is because the gluten helps with binding and gives dough a pleasant texture. Xanthan gum prevents our healthier creations from tasting dense and crumbly. A little goes a long way with xanthan gum, and having it as part of your healthy pantry makes all the difference. I also use a generous pinch of xanthan gum in my smoothies, as it helps to transform them into more authentic milkshakes. Try blending 250 ml/1 cup non-dairy milk, a handful of ice, a handful of frozen fruit, eg mango, blueberries or strawberries, ½ banana and ½ teaspoon xanthan gum – you'll be surprised how great it is. You can also add a handful of spinach to effortlessly sneak some extra greens into your diet; I promise you won't be able to taste it.

Non-dairy milk

We're so lucky to have multiple non-dairy milks available to us nowadays, so it couldn't be easier to go dairy free. I tend to rotate between different options because they all have different nutritional benefits. Rice milk is particularly great for cakes, and I find almond milk is the creamiest so I like to use it for cookies and savoury snacks. Find whichever you prefer and keep a carton in your fridge; you'll see how quickly you go through it – a splash in your tea, a cup in your smoothie, another cup for a recipe. Non-dairy milks tend to keep for 5 days after opening if kept refrigerated, as a general rule.

Apple cider vinegar

Apple cider vinegar is really useful in baking as it helps to activate bicarbonate of/ baking soda. Bicarbonate of/baking soda needs to be mixed with an acid to work, otherwise it won't fulfil its role as efficiently. Apple cider vinegar is a really good choice of acid because when mixed with non-dairy milk, it creates a kind of "buttermilk" so it provides double benefits for your baked goods.

Sweeteners

There are plenty of healthier alternatives to sugar out there; in order to cover your bases it's definitely a good idea to find both a liquid sweetener and a granulated sweetener that you like, because they behave differently when cooked. Where a conventional recipe calls for white sugar for example, using agave syrup in its place will affect the moisture and texture of the finished product. Alternative sweeteners have all been criticized at some point for not being as healthy as they claim, but it's important to remember that these are meant to be used in moderation and regarded as a "treat" food. Use your head, do your research and choose minimally processed wherever possible. My favourite sweeteners? Coconut (palm) sugar and maple syrup.

Xanthan gum

Non-dairy milk

Apple cider vinegar

Coconut sugar

Pure maple syrup

Ground flaxseeds/ linseeds

Eggs are probably the hardest ingredient to replace in healthy cooking. Mix ground flaxseeds/linseeds with water though, and you will be shocked at how similar the texture becomes after a few minutes. This is a "flax egg" and it's invaluable. It can be done for any recipe that calls for eggs – for every egg, sub in 1 tablespoon ground flaxseeds/linseeds mixed with 3 times the amount of water and left until it thickens. You can grind the flaxseeds/linseeds yourself or buy them ready ground, but keep them in your fridge once exposed to air as they spoil easily.

Chia seeds

Much like flaxseeds/linseeds, you can grind these seeds in a coffee grinder or spice grinder and make a "chia egg" to replace regular eggs in baking. Mix 1 tablespoon ground chia and 3 tablespoons water. They are a fantastic source of Omega-3 fatty acids, which is perhaps the most important nutrient to proactively include in our diets (I try to consume at least 1 tablespoon flaxseeds/ linseeds, hemp seeds, or chia seeds per day, and it's particularly important for kids as it's crucial for their brain development).

Coconut oil

You probably know by now that all things "coconut" are super good for us. For instance, the oil is antibacterial, antiviral and antimicrobial, as well as having thyroid-regulating abilities which in turn can positively affect our metabolism. I especially love it for cooking because it's a stable oil, meaning that its molecular structure doesn't change or break down at high temperatures. Other healthy oils such as flax and hemp are much more fragile and heating them can create harmful compounds. I save those oils, along with chia oil and avocado oil, for drizzling on salads and veggies, and use coconut where cooking and baking are involved.

Apple purée/ applesauce

Using apple purée/applesauce helps make up for the moisture lost when you bake without eggs. It also helps you keep the levels of fats in check, because often people will go overboard on the fats in healthified recipes just because they don't want them to come out dry and tasteless. If you want to lower the fat in a conventional recipe that you love, you can always halve the fat and sub in apple purée/applesauce for the other half. It's fairly easy to buy jarred apple purée/ applesauce (make sure it's unsweetened), but you can of course make your own. Feel free to substitute pear purée if you like, too.

Dark/bittersweet chocolate

Most people assume they can't have chocolate when trying to clean up their eats. I wouldn't be able to stay on track if this were the case as I'm a self-confessed chocoholic. You'll find that most dark/bittersweet chocolate that contains 70% cocoa solids is dairy free, so the only thing you have to worry about is what it's sweetened with. Nowadays there are plenty of brands that use xylitol, stevia, and various kinds of fruit sugars in their chocolates. I like chocolate chips best for baking purposes, and they melt really easily too.

Ground flaxseeds/ linseeds

Chia seeds

Coconut oil

Apple purée/ applesauce

Dark/bittersweet chocolate chips

Tips and tricks I've learned along the way

Baking is a fickle thing: It's a very precise science with so many variables, and it can go wrong even when it seems you have followed the instructions to the letter. Every ingredient plays a role in not only taste but also texture, how quickly something cooks, the way it binds, and moisture too. Tweak one tiny thing and everything can change. Here are a few helpful nuggets I learned through my baking adventures that may help you too.

Weights and measures

For cakes, cookies and other baked goods, I really recommend you use cup and tablespoon measures. I have found that measuring ingredients by volume rather than weight leaves less room for mistakes. Measuring with cups also makes it easier to substitute say, a certain amount of agave syrup for the equivalent in maple syrup. If you were doing this by weight there would be no easy way to figure out how much to use, whereas volume-wise, you need exactly the same amount.

To properly measure out a dry ingredient with cup measures, scoop the measure into the dry ingredient, or spoon said ingredient loosely into the cup, and level off the top with a knife. You never want the cup to be tightly packed.

Using exact teaspoon and tablespoon measures really can make all the difference when it comes to using baking powder, bicarbonate of/baking soda, cornflour/cornstarch, arrowroot and xanthan gum. A little goes a long way with all these ingredients so it's important to get it right. If you don't have a teaspoon and tablespoon measure, you can measure out 5 ml and 15 ml respectively. Where these aren't as important are in using things like salt and spices, because if you go a little under or over with your amounts of these, you're not going to affect the overall texture of your baked goods.

Oven temperatures

No two ovens heat to the same temperatures at the same rate. For this reason, preheating your oven to the prescribed temperature is no guarantee things will turn out the way they're meant to. Feel free to keep your goods baking for a little while longer than the recommended time if you think they need it, and remove them before the prescribed time if they look done to you.

There are other factors that affect oven temperature too, such as how often you open the oven door while something is baking (which you should keep to a minimum, for best results), and how long the oven door is open when you put the cake pan in. Complicated, I know. Additionally, the way your mixture bakes will be different depending on whether you put it in 10 minutes after you preheated the oven, or 15 minutes after. Using an oven thermometer will help make matters more precise and less variable.

When you are baking cakes or other mixtures and it seems like the outside is already cooked but the inside still needs a little more time, simply cover the top of your cake pan with a sheet of foil and continue baking. This will prevent the outside from overcooking while allowing the inside to warm.

16

Substituting ingredients

In almost all of the recipes in this book, you can use non-dairy milks interchangeably. So for example if a recipe calls for almond milk and you only have rice milk on hand or prefer to use hazelnut milk, you can usually do so and the recipe will come out the same way as intended. The same goes for liquid sweeteners – I love to use maple syrup, but you can use agave syrup, brown rice syrup or honey according to your preferences and your needs. When baking though, you can't substitute a liquid sweetener for a granulated sweetener or vice versa.

When it comes to granulated sweeteners, there's a little wiggle room in substituting one for the other, but it's worth remembering that stevia is a lot sweeter than fruit sugar (such as Fruisana), coconut sugar and xylitol, which are in turn sweeter than white sugar, so you're safer sticking to xylitol or fruit sugar when the recipe calls for it. The other thing about stevia is that it can taste a little weird when cooked. For this reason I tend to reserve it for cold drinks and foods that have to be refrigerated or frozen to set. You can feel free to use fruit sugar, xylitol, palm sugar and coconut sugar interchangeably though. The latter two have a caramel-like taste that you can use to alter taste where you like. For example I think the Nanaimo bars taste much better when I use coconut sugar over xylitol.

Perhaps the hardest ingredient to substitute effectively is flour. This is because flour can be made from almost any grain, bean or nut, all of which cook at varying rates. Where a recipe calls for chickpea flour and you sub it for brown rice flour, it may make all the difference between a gorgeous cake and a chalky mess. You also run the risk of the flour cooking way faster or slower than the other ingredients involved, which doesn't make for good results taste-wise. I recommend looking for a good gluten-free plain/all-purpose flour to use where grain flours are called for. If you are keen to see how a particular flour you love would work in a recipe though, you can play around with things – in fact that's half the fun! You just have to be open to trying and tweaking a couple of times before you reach your desired outcome.

When a recipe calls for almond flour for example, it's fine to swap it out for another nut flour; that shouldn't cause too many problems. It's worth noting though that ground almonds/almond meal and almond flour are not interchangeable. Though they are technically both almonds that have been ground, ground almonds/almond meal are coarser and less even in texture. This is what you would get when you process almonds in your food processor at home. Almond flour, on the other hand, is finer and drier and difficult to replicate at home in terms of texture, so if a recipe calls for almond flour I would recommend purchasing some.

For savoury and non-baking recipes, it's particularly easy – and usually successful! – to ring the changes and experiment with the nuts, seeds, fruits and vegetables you happen to have to hand. Be brave and work with what you have!

Bicarbonate of/baking soda

Bicarbonate of/baking soda starts to react as soon as it's mixed with wet ingredients. For this reason, when you're working with a recipe that calls for bicarbonate of/baking soda, it's important that you are speedy at getting the mixture in the oven once all the ingredients have been combined. The same does not apply to baking powder.

Whisking

I used to think that whisking dry ingredients together meant beating them really fast with an electric whisk. Not the case! I later learned that all this means is stirring them together with a balloon whisk. This helps incorporate the ingredients more effectively than stirring with a spoon. I often use the dry whisk technique in place of sifting as it works just as well, but is less laborious.

Breakfasts

It is well documented that breakfast is the most important meal of the day but many of us fall into the trap of being in too much of a hurry to drink or eat anything as we fly out of the door to start the day. Making granola for the week (with only good stuff, not added sugar like in the storebought varieties), or preparing apple pie oatmeal the night before will ensure that you get a super-tasty bowl of fuel that will send you skipping to work and keep you sustained until lunchtime. Swap your children's bowl of cereal for a plate of quick-to-make protein pancakes and you'll know that you're cutting out the preservatives, refined sugars and artificial vitamins that so often come with packaged breakfast food.

Orange, cardamom and hemp-seed muffins

Makes 24 mini muffins, or about
9–10 regular muffins

125 g/1 cup quinoa flour
½ teaspoon bicarbonate of/
  baking soda
1 teaspoon baking powder
½ teaspoon salt
1 teaspoon ground cardamom
1 teaspoon ground cinnamon
2–3 big tablespoons shelled
  hemp seeds
1–1½ teaspoons orange extract
  or orange oil
1 tablespoon apple cider vinegar
85 ml/⅓ cup unsweetened apple
  purée/applesauce
60 ml/¼ cup rice or almond milk
3 tablespoons pure maple syrup,
  or more apple purée/applesauce
2 tablespoons granulated
  sweetener

*24-hole mini muffin pan, lined with
(eco-friendly) paper cases*

As a teenager, I went through a phase of being obsessed with coffee-shop breakfast muffins, but even before I knew much about healthy eating, I used to notice feeling light-headed from the sugar crash that came after eating them, and hungry long before lunch.

I still love the idea of starting the day with warm baked goods though, especially when it's cold outside. I wanted to create a muffin that was healthy enough to be considered a "power breakfast", with plenty of protein and healthy Omega-3 fats from quinoa flour and hemp seeds, as well as minimal sugar. These are therefore considerably less sweet than a "treat" muffin, but heavy on flavour thanks to warming notes of cardamom and cinnamon, mixed with the pop of the orange.

I created these as mini muffins so you can decide how substantial you want your snack to be, and also because, well, they're cuter. Have three or four for breakfast with an apple and a hot drink, grab a couple for elevenses, or pop a few in your kids' lunchboxes. If you make a batch at the beginning of the week, your morning eats will be a no-brainer until Friday.

Preheat the oven to 180°C (350°F) Gas 4.

In a bowl, combine the quinoa flour, bicarbonate of/baking soda, baking powder and salt, then sift in the cardamom and cinnamon. Add a generous portion of the shelled hemp seeds. There's no need to measure these – more hemp seeds will amp up the protein and healthy fats in your muffins.

Separately, mix together the orange extract, vinegar, apple purée, milk, maple syrup and sweetener.

Mix the wet ingredients into the bowl of dry ingredients, but be sure not to overmix everything. Spoon the mixture into the muffin cases, filling them just three-quarters full, and level the tops with your index finger. Bake in the preheated oven for 8–10 minutes for mini muffins, and 9–12 minutes for regular muffins. It's fine to slightly under-bake these if you want them to be particularly moist on the inside because none of the ingredients involved are harmful if consumed raw.

Allow the muffins to cool for 4 minutes before tasting. Store in an airtight container for up to 5 days.

Power protein granola

Serves 8

275 g/1½ cups buckwheat groats
170 g/1 cup cooked quinoa
3 tablespoons chia seeds (see page 44 for information about these)
35 g/¼ cup pumpkin seeds
40 g/¼ cup almonds, roughly chopped
2 teaspoons ground cinnamon
½ teaspoon grated nutmeg
1 teaspoon vanilla extract
60 ml/¼ cup coconut oil
60 ml/¼ cup pure maple syrup
3 tablespoons water (optional)

baking sheet lined with baking parchment or foil

I so named this recipe because it contains the three most "superfood-y" ingredients in the grain and seed category – chia seeds, buckwheat and quinoa. Granola is a food often associated with being healthy but most of the time granolas contain ridiculous amounts of sugar. Even healthier versions of it can be too heavy if they are made primarily with nuts, which means you can't really have a bowl's worth of the stuff. This version contains only about 4 tablespoons maple syrup for the entire batch, and no other added sugars in the form of dried fruits. It also has a high protein content too, since buckwheat, quinoa and chia seeds are composed of 13, 15, and 20 percent protein respectively.

I often fill a mason jar with this granola and gift it to clients for special occasions, and it always receives rave reviews.

Preheat the oven to 180°C (350°F) Gas 4.

In a large bowl, mix the buckwheat groats, quinoa, chia seeds, pumpkin seeds, almonds, cinnamon and nutmeg.

Put the vanilla extract, coconut oil and maple syrup in a saucepan over low heat and allow to melt. Now pour it into the bowl of dry ingredients and toss to coat. Add the water if you prefer your granola a little less crunchy.

Spread the granola out on the prepared baking sheet, and don't worry if there are clumps. Bake in the preheated oven for about 1 hour.

When it has cooled for a few minutes, break it apart into clusters.

Store in a cool place in an airtight container for up to 3 weeks.

Serve with dairy-free milk and fresh fruit, eg blueberries.

Did you know?
Back when I was first getting into healthy foods, I stayed away from using buckwheat because I assumed it was a kind of wheat. In reality, it's not even a cereal grain but the seed of a fruit closely related to rhubarb. It's totally gluten free, and also low-GI, high in protein (25%), and rich in magnesium, which we could all do with more of. You can buy the groats (kernels) in bulk, or buy buckwheat flour to use in your healthy baking adventures. When I go out to eat Japanese food, I often choose a soba noodle dish because these are made from buckwheat. A soba dish feels comforting and indulgent and is still a lot healthier than plenty of the sushi options.

Popcorn parfaits

Makes 1

2 teaspoons corn kernels
1 teaspoon xylitol or stevia
125–150 g/²⁄₃–¾ cup dairy-free
   yogurt (I recommend Coyo
   dairy-free coconut yogurt)
1 teaspoon pumpkin seeds,
   or your seeds of choice
80–100 g/¾ cup mixed berries
   of choice
agave syrup, for drizzling (optional)

1 tall glass

Popcorn is a health-conscious person's best friend. It is a whole grain, very low in calories, and SO much fun to eat. Did you know it also has almost twice the antioxidant levels of most fruits too? It's a shame then, that most of us only think of it as an afternoon snack or a cinema treat. Why not use it where we would use other whole grains as part of a healthy breakfast?

Think of making popcorn for breakfast the same way you would think about cooking some quick stovetop oatmeal – buy it in bulk and let it last you for weeks. As an added bonus, it takes even less time to prepare too!

Try this popcorn parfait once and love it forever.

Put the corn kernels and sweetener in a non-stick saucepan over medium heat and place the lid on top. As soon as you hear the corn start to pop, turn the heat down to low. Remove when all corn has popped – about 45–60 seconds. Allow the popcorn to cool slightly.

Mix together the yogurt and seeds. Place half at the bottom of your tall glass, then layer half of the berries and half of the popcorn. Repeat these layers once more, and drizzle with agave syrup if you wish.

Apple pie oatmeal
with coconut whip

Serves 1

40 g/½ cup oats (rolled or whole/
    jumbo oats rather than the
    "quick cook" versions)
120–160 ml/⅔–¾ cup unsweetened
    apple purée/applesauce,
    depending on how thick you
    want your oatmeal
½ teaspoon ground cinnamon
½ teaspoon grated nutmeg
splash of almond milk
6–7 walnuts, coarsely chopped

Coconut whip
400-ml/14-oz. can of coconut milk,
    refrigerated for at least 2 hours
    (don't use light or low-fat
    coconut milk as these won't
    work in this recipe)
1–2 tablespoons xylitol or stevia,
    or other granulated sweetener
dash of vanilla extract

The benefits of eating porridge for breakfast are well known. As a child though, I always found the obligatory bowl of oats quite boring. I would spruce it up by eating it cold, made with apple juice instead of water or milk. This apple pie-flavoured oatmeal evolved from there. You can eat it as is on a hurried weekday morning, or if you have more time to enjoy it, top it with coconut whip for a really special breakfast. Please note that the oatmeal recipe needs to be started the day before you want to serve it.

The day before you want to serve the oatmeal, combine the oats and apple purée/applesauce in a bowl, cover it and refrigerate it overnight. The oats will soak up the apple and expand, so when you take your mixture out in the morning it will be nice and thick.

The next morning, put the soaked oatmeal in a saucepan over low–medium heat, stir in the cinnamon and nutmeg and heat it up very gently. Once hot, spoon the oatmeal into a bowl. Add a splash of cold milk – the contrast between the hot and cold is really delicious.

Top the oatmeal with walnuts, plus some coconut whip if using. Serve!

For the coconut whip
Open the can of chilled coconut milk, being careful not to shake it. A thick layer of coconut "cream" should have formed on the surface of the milk and on the lid. Scrape this off and place in a bowl – this is the part you need to make the whip. Add enough sweetener and vanilla extract to taste – the coconut is sweet on its own, so you just need a little of these to bring out its natural flavours. Beat with an electric whisk until the mixture resembles whipped cream – this can take up to about 6 minutes.

Store any leftover coconut whip in an airtight container in the fridge for up to 3 days, and feel free to whisk it again if the texture doesn't hold up as desired.

You can serve coconut whip as an accompaniment to cakes, ice cream and pies.

Breakfast salad

Serves 1

2 heads of Baby Gem lettuce
(or 2 large handfuls of any greens
you like; I would recommend
Cos lettuce or Baby Gem if
you're trying it for the first time,
and spinach or chard if you fancy
experimenting afterwards)
1 large banana
1 orange
1 large tablespoon shelled
hemp seeds
1 tablespoon unsweetened
desiccated coconut

Dressing
1 orange
1 tablespoon peanut butter

This is less of a recipe and more of a blueprint for you to create your own bright, juicy start to the day. Salad does sound like an odd idea for breakfast, I'll admit, but you just have to try it once to be converted. You'll notice that this a BIG salad, but don't be afraid of the portion size because it's all alkalizing, fresh, raw goodness.

Chop the lettuce, banana and orange and put in a large bowl. Add the hemp seeds and coconut.

For the dressing
Squeeze the juice from the orange and whisk it with the peanut butter until completely smooth.

Drizzle the dressing over the salad to serve.

Variation
1 head of Baby Gem lettuce, 2 mangoes, 10-cm/4-inch piece of cucumber (sliced into rounds), 2 tablespoons almonds (chopped). For the dressing, 60 g/½ cup raspberries blended with 1 tablespoon pure maple syrup.

Protein pancakes

Serves 1

6 tablespoons gluten-free plain/
   all-purpose flour of choice
1 scoop of protein powder
   of choice
½ tablespoon xylitol or stevia,
   or other granulated sweetener
½ teaspoon baking powder
a pinch of salt
1 small banana
1 tablespoon non-dairy milk
   of choice
1 teaspoon vanilla extract
½ teaspoon coconut oil
berries of choice and maple syrup,
   or dark/bittersweet chocolate
   chips, to serve

Who doesn't love a pancake? With a healthifying makeover, you can have these any day of the week rather than saving them for an indulgent Sunday brunch. Sometimes, when I'm wiped out at the end of the day, I whip these up for dinner and I never feel guilty about it…

In a bowl, combine the flour, protein powder, sweetener, baking powder and salt.

Separately, mash the banana until no lumps remain, then add the milk and vanilla extract.

Mix the wet ingredients into the bowl of dry ingredients until well combined.

Melt the coconut oil in a frying pan over medium heat so that it coats the bottom of the pan. Spoon a quarter of the pancake batter at a time into the pan, then flip the pancake over when you see it start to bubble. Cook until golden underneath. Remove the pancake from the pan and keep it warm while you make the remaining pancakes with the rest of the batter.

Serve with berries and a touch of maple syrup for a healthy option, or dark/bittersweet chocolate chips for a treat.

Did you know?
Protein is the "It" nutrient right now, and as a result protein powders have sprouted up all over the place. However, many of them are comprised of cheap fillers and as a result can be more of a hinderance than a help to our bodies. Often, they are sweetened with sugar or worse, artificial sweeteners like aspartame, which comes in many different disguises.

   Look for a plain, natural protein such as hemp, pea, sprouted brown rice, or quinoa, ideally with 10 ingredients or fewer; as a rule of thumb stay away from anything with the word "isolate" in the ingredients. Also, the more novel the flavour of the protein powder (eg cookies and cream, peanut butter and jam), the more processed it is likely to be. I recommend you buy either plain, vanilla or chocolate and tweak the flavours with ingredients from your kitchen. Some brands I love: Good Hemp Food, Naturya, Tempt, Vega and Sunwarrior.

Fruit frosties

Mango and
blueberry

Papaya and lime

Pineapple and
blood orange

Fruit has been getting a bad rap lately, with a lot of people advising that we cut out sugary fruits if we want to lose weight. The way I think of it, we have been eating fruit since the beginning of mankind, and it's actually the BEST food for weight management, as well as energy and vitality. It's full of the fibre, hydration, vitamins and minerals we require; moreover, it passes quickly through our system and is the least taxing food on our digestion, so we have no problem getting all the goodness from it with very minimal energy. It gives us the sugar we are wired to crave, because that is the fuel every cell in our bodies runs on. I have found that eating fruit in abundance often seems to be the solution to some clients' struggle with omnipresent sugar cravings. I usually start my mornings with a large dose of fruit, eat until my body has had enough, and then I have something more substantial if and when my body tells me it's hungry again.

Eating fruit is the simple part; the difficult part is making sure the fruit you fancy eating on any given morning is perfectly ripe. Off-season fruit is also very expensive, and hard to find in organic form. The solution to this is to freeze large amounts of seasonal fruit when you can get your hands on it, and then blend up these fun frosty drinks in whichever combinations you feel like, whenever you feel like them. They are a delicious and fun way to get your vitamins, especially when you're on the go. They make a great after-school snack for kids too.

Blood oranges are a great example of fruit in season during the winter months, which shows you that summer isn't the only time for a high-fruit diet. In fact most citrus is at its tastiest in winter, and the same goes for pomegranates, pears and sharon fruit (also known as kaki or persimmon), to name a few.

The key to a good frosty is a high-speed blender specially equipped to cope with ice and which will be strong enough to break down frozen fruit until smooth and creamy.

N.B. Before you start blending, it helps to let your frozen fruit thaw for 4–5 minutes, and feel free to add a splash of water to help the fruit whizz round. You may have to scrape down the insides of the blender as you go.

For 1 papaya and lime frosty
Scoop out the flesh of 1 large papaya (or 2 small ones) and freeze in a sandwich bag overnight. Blitz in a high-speed blender with the juice of 1 lime until smooth.

For 1 pineapple and blood orange frosty
Cut 1 sweet, ripe pineapple into chunks and freeze in a sandwich bag overnight (you can also use pre-cut frozen pineapple). Blitz half of the pineapple chunks (about 2 big handfuls) in a high-speed blender with the juice of 3 blood oranges until smooth.

For 1 mango and blueberry frosty
Cut 3 mangoes into chunks and freeze in a sandwich bag overnight (you can also use pre-cut frozen mango). Blitz with a large handful of fresh or frozen blueberries in a high-speed blender until smooth.

Power Snacks

Spirulina, dates, goji berries, cashews, hemp seeds, coconut oil, chia, maca, sesame seeds – these are just some of the ingredients you'll encounter on your mission to pep up your energy stores. All of the ideas in this chapter are packed with natural sugars, protein and nutrient-rich fruits, nuts and seeds to ensure that your body is getting easily absorbed, long-lasting and sustaining energy whether you're a fitness fanatic or you just need a pick-me-up. And there's no need to snack on peanut butter and toast any more – you can make your own range of far superior nut butters.

Frozen popsicles

On the whole I find the idea of pouring fruit juice into an ice lolly mould kind of uninspiring. But what if you were to elevate the whole concept of fun–but–healthy snacking by sneaking some veggies into sweet, exotic ice pops? Here are my two favourite green smoothies turned into fun treats for both kids and adults. These taste far from virtuous, so feel free to serve them to guests who will be none the wiser.

Orange-creamsicle pops

Makes 4–6

I ripe banana
freshly squeezed juice of 3 oranges
  (about 250 ml/1 cup)
¼ avocado
250 ml/1 cup coconut milk
  (or almond milk if you prefer)
dash of vanilla extract

4–6 ice lolly/pop moulds

In 2012 I came up with an orange creamsicle-flavoured smoothie and went through a phase of having it every day for breakfast. On one of the handful of days that it was actually hot that summer, there were some ice lolly/pop moulds on display in my local grocery store. I bought them on impulse and the orange creamsicle smoothie was the first thing I poured into them.

Put all the ingredients in a blender and blitz until smooth.

Divide between the ice lolly/pop moulds. Freeze until frozen through.

Green juice pops

Makes 4–6

½ cucumber
300 g/about 2 cups chopped
  pineapple, fresh or frozen
generous handful of fresh
  flat-leaf parsley
small handful of spinach (optional,
  but the taste is undetectable
  so don't let it put you off)
I lime
I teaspoon stevia
½ teaspoon spirulina powder

4–6 ice lolly/pop moulds

This is my favourite green smoothie of all time. It tastes good enough to be a cocktail, and has transformed even the biggest green-juice sceptics I've met. It's hard to imagine how delicious it is until you actually make it, especially when you look at the ingredients list. It makes the perfect refresher for a summer afternoon, and as an added bonus the greens will help sustain your energy levels through until dinner.

Put the cucumber, pineapple, parsley and spinach, if using, in a blender. Blitz until smooth, then squeeze in either half or the whole lime, depending on how tart you want your ice pops to taste. If making these for kids, I'd recommend using only half of the lime. Add the stevia and spirulina and blitz again to mix.

Divide between the ice lolly/pop moulds. Freeze until frozen through.

On-the-go snack bars

Makes 4

2 scoops of protein powder
of choice
60 ml/¼ cup canned, unsweetened
puréed pumpkin
60 ml/¼ cup almond butter (drain
off the oil before measuring)
xylitol or stevia, to taste (optional)
6 tablespoons buckwheat groats

baking dish, about 23 x 10 cm/
9 x 4 inches, lightly greased
with coconut oil

You know those protein bars that seem like a dream come true because they come in "cookies and cream" or "peanut butter" flavour, are only 200 calories and contain 16+ grams protein? It's so easy to think they are good for us because of the clever marketing, whereas in reality most of them are full of isolated ingredients synthesized unnaturally in a lab. Those calories aren't ones that our bodies recognize, that protein is denatured and thus unusable, and as for the flavourings, they are like a chemical storm as far as our systems are concerned.

Having said that, what the bars DO have in their favour is convenience. These homemade versions take less than 5 minutes to prepare and can be kept in your freezer for up to 3 weeks at a time, so that you never need to be stuck for a protein-rich snack.

Put the protein powder, pumpkin and almond butter in a bowl and mix to combine. Add sweetener to taste – I find that the protein powder and pumpkin make it plenty sweet on its own, but adjust it so that it tastes good to you. Stir in the buckwheat groats.

Spoon the mixture into the prepared baking dish, level it out with the back of a spoon and freeze for at least 1 hour.

Just to show you that you can match the commercial bars for protein with all-natural ingredients, check out these stats per bar:
Protein powder: 8 g (based on 1 bar being 16 g)
Almond butter: 2.5 g
Buckwheat groats: 3 g
Pumpkin: 0.75 g
= more than 14 g total protein per bar

Coconut and spirulina energy bites

Makes about 16

90 g/½ cup dates, stoned
65 g/½ cup cashews
1 large teaspoon coconut oil
1½–2 teaspoons spirulina powder
1 large teaspoon matcha powder
  (green tea powder)
about 20 g/¼ cup unsweetened
  desiccated coconut

1 small cup half filled with water

Spirulina is possibly the least palatable of the superfoods, and clients often complain to me that they hate the taste, no matter how they try to mask it. However, it's also one of those things that we know is good for us, even though we often don't know why.

When I was first diagnosed with candida and hormonal imbalances by a nutritionist, the first thing she prescribed was a daily dose of spirulina powder mixed into water, as it's a very powerful alkalizer. Alkalizing foods help bring the body to its "happy place" where it can function at its best, so she was hoping it would help my body to correct its own ailments. At the time I didn't understand the reasoning, and the spirulina water tasted so disgusting I was pretty bad at keeping it up.

When I eventually understood all the benefits of spirulina, I came up with this recipe to give us all an easier and much more delicious way to eat it.

Soak the dates in a bowl of water for 30 minutes, but no longer than that.

Put the cashews in a food processor fitted with an "S" blade and pulse for about 30–45 seconds until a thick meal has formed.

Rinse the dates, wipe off any extra moisture and add them to the food processor along with the coconut oil, spirulina and matcha powder. Process until a large ball starts to form. Remove the blade and take the processor bowl off the stand.

Using the prepared cup of water to wet your hands as you go, pinch off pieces of the mixture about the size of whole walnuts. Roll them into balls between the palms of your hands. (Damp hands will stop the mixture sticking too much.)

Roll each ball in the desiccated coconut to coat it evenly, then place on a plate or board. Repeat with the rest of the mixture.

Refrigerate the energy bites for at least 20 minutes. Store in the fridge in an airtight container for up to 3 weeks.

Sports bites

Makes 8

50 g/½ cup raw almonds (use raw
   ones if you can, to make this an
   all-raw recipe)
60 g/½ cup dried apricots
   (preferably unsulfured)
2 tablespoons shelled hemp seeds
1½ tablespoons coconut oil
vanilla extract

These sports bites were created for a group of 21 adventurers, including wounded servicemen, who trekked across the North Pole in 2011. The trip's organizer asked me to create a small, compact source of energy that the group could easily stop to eat at regular intervals during the trek. I knew that the ideal snack for them needed some natural fruit sugars for energy as well as some kind of nut for protein. After playing around with different combinations, I decided that apricots with almonds was the tastiest combination. I then added coconut oil and hemp seeds for their healthy fats, which benefit skin health and act as lubricants for our joints. Hemp seeds in particular are a fantastic source of Omega-3 fatty acids, and the coconut oil is antibacterial and helps regulate metabolism.

After the group came back with rave reviews, I started making these as compact workout snacks and they became really popular. Unlike the commercial protein bars that are marketed as exercise fuel, these are light and can be eaten in two bites, but still provide that little boost we need.

Put the almonds in a food processor fitted with an "S" blade and pulse until crumbly. Add the apricots and process until well incorporated and the mixture starts to come together into a paste. Add the hemp seeds and coconut oil, plus vanilla extract to taste.

Divide the mixture into 8 and roll each portion into a ball between the palms of your hands.

Freeze the sports bites for at least 15 minutes. Store in the fridge in an airtight container for up to 3 weeks.

Chia shots

Makes 4

4 teaspoons chia seeds
1 fresh mint leaf, or ½ tablespoon
  dried mint
1 lime
½ lemon
1 teaspoon stevia

coffee grinder or spice grinder
4 shot glasses

Chia seeds are the new superfood in town. Bursting with health-promoting nutrients like calcium and magnesium, Omega-3 fatty acids and plant protein, they are as "complete" as a food can be. However they are not the easiest things to incorporate into your daily eats, as they absorb about 8 times their weight in water so they should be soaked before consuming. You could make a chia pudding with them for breakfast, but since they make such perfect workout fuel, these servings in a shot are an easy way to consume them when you need a quick energy boost on the go.

Using a coffee or spice grinder, grind the chia seeds and mint leaf together until they have formed a fine meal. Divide the mixture between 4 shot glasses, then squeeze in a little lime and lemon juice.

Fill the shot glasses to the top with water. Divide the stevia between each glass and stir to mix. Refrigerate for at least 10 minutes to allow the chia to expand in the liquid.

Stir vigorously before serving. Take it in a shot like you would vodka!

Did you know?

These shots are based on the "iskiate" or "chia fresca" drunk by the Native American Tarahumara tribe for sustenance. It was said the Tarahumarans ran long distances as a way of life, sometimes 50 miles a day, and chia seeds were their preferred source of energy. Supposedly they would carry dry chia seeds on 24-hour marches to keep them going, or they would drink "chia fresca", which is still a well-known concoction in Central and South America. It is made by combining a large glass of water, a teaspoon of chia seeds, some lemon juice and sugar. Think of "chia fresca" as an afternoon snack which you can easily healthify by swapping the sugar for maple syrup or agave syrup, and the chia shots as a turbocharger for your workouts or runs. They give those storebought energy gels a run for their money!

Chia pudding

People often ask me, if I don't consume any dairy, where do I get my calcium from? If I don't eat any oily fish, where do I get my Omega-3 fatty acids from? If I don't eat meat, how do I get my protein? In one answer, chia seeds! These tiny little powerhouses contain all three of these beneficial substances, in plentiful amounts to boot.

With chia seeds, a little goes a long way; you need just one tablespoon for a serving (see previous recipe for more information). When left to sit in liquid, they expand and form a gel-like pudding; the seeds themselves are tasteless so the pudding will take on whatever flavour you give the liquid. Get creative! Chia pudding is a great alternative to oatmeal in the morning, as it's very filling and also less starchy.

Each recipe serves 1

Autumn-spiced chia pudding

1 tablespoon chia seeds
100 ml/6 tablespoons almond milk
freshly squeezed juice of 1 carrot
¼ teaspoon ground ginger
¼ teaspoon ground cloves
¼ teaspoon grated nutmeg
½ teaspoon ground cinnamon
1 tablespoon pure maple syrup,
    agave syrup or coconut nectar

Put the chia seeds and milk in an airtight container and stir well to combine, making sure there are no clumps. Set aside for 10 minutes – the seeds will start to expand.

Add the remaining ingredients, stir again, and refrigerate: for 1 hour if you like it thin, or overnight if you like it thick and comforting, almost like oatmeal.

Vanilla and coconut chia pudding

1 tablespoon chia seeds
125 ml/½ cup almond milk
3 tablespoons unsweetened
    desiccated coconut
1 teaspoon vanilla extract

Put the chia seeds and milk in an airtight container and stir well to combine, making sure there are no clumps. Set aside for 10 minutes – the seeds will start to expand.

Add the remaining ingredients, stir again, and refrigerate: for 1 hour if you like it thin, or overnight if you like it thick and comforting, almost like oatmeal.

Chocolate chia pudding

1 tablespoon chia seeds
125 ml/½ cup almond milk
1½ tablespoons unsweetened
    cocoa powder
2 tablespoons pure maple syrup

Put the chia seeds and milk in an airtight container and stir well to combine, making sure there are no clumps. Set aside for 10 minutes – the seeds will start to expand.

Add the remaining ingredients, stir again, and refrigerate: for 1 hour if you like it thin, or overnight if you like it thick and comforting, almost like oatmeal. I keep it in my fridge (for up to 5 days) and steal a few spoonfuls when I need a little sweet pick-me-up.

Cocoa-almond freezer fudge pops

Makes 8

70 ml/¼ cup almond butter (drain off the oil before measuring)
2 teaspoons ground flaxseeds/linseeds
1 large teaspoon coconut oil
1 large teaspoon xylitol
1½ tablespoons unsweetened cocoa powder (preferably raw), plus extra for dusting
½ teaspoon vanilla extract
for an extra boost, add 1 teaspoon espresso powder

This is a frozen, chocolatey nut butter concoction that I made up one day when I was really craving dark/bittersweet chocolate. It's very common for women to crave chocolate at certain points in their cycles: what we're actually lacking is a hit of magnesium, which helps regulate the nervous system and aids sleep too.

Chocolate is never something I've felt I had to give up in my quest to be healthy, but there are definitely ways to "upgrade" your chocolate fix. I pop one of these frozen treats into my mouth when I know my body will be satisfied with a hit of pure cocoa. If you can find raw cocoa powder, use it in this recipe as its potency is greater than that of regular cocoa powder.

Put all the ingredients in a food processor and blitz until smooth.

Divide the mixture into 8 and roll each portion into a ball between the palms of your hands. Dust in cocoa powder.

Freeze the fudge pops for at least 30 minutes and consume straight from the freezer. Store in the freezer for up to 4 weeks.

Did you know?

So many of us are stuck in a cycle of restricting and bingeing when it comes to food, and it can seem impossible to find a different way. I tell my clients that in order to eat healthily in the long-term, they have to make it about more than being slim. This myopic view will keep you in that destructive tug-of-war. For me, things started to shift and settle when I learned to eat from a place of self-love rather than self-loathing. When you eat with the consciousness of treating yourself with the utmost respect and gratitude, the battle between being "good" and "bad" seems to disappear.

Nut and seed butters

My journey to eating healthier couldn't have been done without nut and seed butters. I had been told in the past that a handful of nuts makes a good snack along with a piece of fruit. There are only so many days you can do that before you feel uninspired. Once you give those nuts a whirr around the food processor and flavour them with other delicious ingredients, you've suddenly got a smooth, creamy paste that you can smear on an apple and it'll transform it into something more exciting. Nut butters are also really versatile sources of healthy fat that you can include into almost any meal imaginable.

I love my daily dose of nut butter, which helps ensure I get those good kinds of fats in my diet. I make sure to rotate a few different homemade varieties so that I get a wide array of all the amazing benefits nuts and seeds have to offer.

Each recipe makes about 8 servings (about 2 tablespoons per serving)

For each recipe, place the nuts and seeds in a food processor fitted with an "S" blade first; initially they will turn into a thick powder, then their natural oils will come through and you'll start to see a "butter" form. Add the remaining ingredients and pulse until creamy and smooth.

N.B. I like the Spicy Sesame Butter on the chunkier side, so I tend to pulse the seeds down for a little less time.

170 g/1 cup almonds
2 teaspoons pure maple syrup
a pinch of salt

Basic almond butter

This oh-so-simple and basic nut butter will probably always be my favourite because of its sheer versatility. Beyond pairing it with yogurt or fruit, you can drizzle it on oatmeal (or on top of the Popcorn Parfaits on page 24!), top a baked sweet potato with 1–2 tablespoons' worth, or mix it with some soy sauce and lemon for a great stir-fry base.

125 g/¾ cup almonds
40 g/¼ cup shelled hemp seeds
½ tablespoon ground cinnamon
1 tablespoon maca powder
   (see page 102 for information
   about this)
½ teaspoon vanilla extract
1 teaspoon xylitol or stevia
2 tablespoons hemp oil (use
   flaxseed/linseed, coconut or
   chia oil if you can't find hemp oil)

Warming maca, cinnamon and hemp-seed almond butter

This is an almond butter variation that I enjoy in the winter because the cinnamon and maca are very warming to the body. With the cooler months, it's very easy for skin to dry out too, so I add a big dose of hemp seeds for their amazing Omega-3 levels, to help keep me moisturized from the inside out. You can pair this with whatever you like, but I love to dunk a big spoon into my jar and eat it straight up.

120 g/1 cup sesame seeds
2 tablespoons ground flaxseeds/
   linseeds
2 tablespoons sesame oil or
   olive oil
1 tablespoon freshly squeezed
   lemon juice, or apple cider
   vinegar
1 tablespoon nutritional yeast
   (optional)
¼ teaspoon sea salt
½–1 teaspoon cayenne pepper

Spicy sesame butter

I've seen plenty of sweet nut butters, and plenty of plain ones. But wouldn't it be great to have a savoury option for when that salty/fatty craving strikes? That way, it would be much easier to resist diving into a bag of chips. Spread this on a few thick cucumber slices, or on a healthy cracker. You could even mix it into cooked vegetables, such as green beans, spinach and red (bell) peppers.

130 g/1 cup pumpkin seeds
1 tablespoon coconut oil
60 ml/¼ cup pure maple syrup
a pinch of salt
1 teaspoon freshly squeezed
   lemon juice
½ teaspoon vanilla extract

Maple and lemon pumpkin-seed butter

I made this on a whim one day, when we had some really sour, crunchy green apples at home. I had envisaged a sweet and tangy nut butter to go with it. At the time I was also trying to increase my zinc intake because everyone around me was getting sick and zinc is amazing for giving our immune systems a boost. So I based the seed butter around pumpkin seeds, which are one of the best dietary sources of this mineral. Most of us are permanently deficient in zinc, and this is a painless way to up your levels.

Paleo cookies

Makes 16 small cookies

2 teaspoons ground chia seeds
  (buy them ready ground, or
  grind whole seeds in a coffee/
  spice grinder)
2 tablespoons water
170 g/1½ cups pecans (see
  instructions below), or
  ground almonds/almond meal
3 tablespoons unsweetened
  desiccated coconut
1 teaspoon ground cinnamon
½ teaspoon grated nutmeg
1 teaspoon baking powder
a pinch of salt
dash of vanilla extract
3 teaspoons stevia
2 tablespoons almond milk

*baking sheet lined with baking
  parchment*

I once received a custom catering request for a client who was on both a paleo and diabetic-friendly diet. This meant she couldn't consume any grain flours, nor could she have any natural sugars like agave, maple syrup or honey – but she was craving cookies! I came up with the idea of making flour out of pecans, which she told me she loves, and completely omitted sugars aside from stevia, which doesn't raise blood sugar levels at all. I was a bit sceptical about making something taste great within all those strict parameters, but she loved them so much I ended up including them in my regular offering. They became one of the most popular choices, with so many people watching their carbohydrate intake nowadays.

These cookies are made with such clean and healthful ingredients that they make an ideal power snack which also feels like a treat. This recipe is for a basic paleo cookie, so feel free to use it as a blueprint and add mix-ins of your choice, such as dried cranberries, scant flaxseeds/linseeds or pumpkin seeds.

Preheat the oven to 180°C (350°F) Gas 4.

Put the ground chia seeds and water in a small bowl. Whisk the seeds into the water with a fork until the mixture starts to feel like the consistency of a beaten egg – in fact, what you have are 2 "chia eggs" that play the same role as eggs in plant-based baking recipes. Place in the refrigerator.

Put the pecans in a food processor and blitz until they have become a fine powder. You don't want to overprocess them, as they will start to form a paste instead. You should end up with 1 cup of flour – make sure you have this much and blitz more pecans if you don't. In a bowl, combine the pecan flour, desiccated coconut, cinnamon, nutmeg, baking powder and salt.

Add the "chia egg", vanilla extract, stevia and almond milk to the bowl of dry ingredients and mix well. Divide the mixture into 16 and shape each portion into balls, then flatten them between your palms to make little cookies. Arrange them on the prepared baking sheet.

Bake in the preheated oven for about 6 minutes. Transfer to a wire to cool completely. Store in an airtight container for up to 4 days.

Party Snacks

Catering for a group of friends is no reason to throw healthiness out of the window! There are so many easy and tasty snacks and treats to be made that will out-do anything you can buy ready-made. Baking and clever seasoning will both happily replace frying and over-salting to produce ultra-imaginative and moreish fingerfood that your friends will be thrilled with. And as a lot of these recipes can be made in advance and stored, you won't find yourself panic-buying bumper packs of potato chips and pretzels on the morning of the party.

Rosemary breadsticks

Makes 12–14

180 ml/¾ cup lukewarm water
1 teaspoon dry quick yeast
½ teaspoon agave syrup
   or honey
300 g/3 cups gluten-free plain/
   all-purpose flour of choice,
   plus extra for dusting
3 teaspoons xanthan gum
1½ teaspoons sea salt
leaves from a few sprigs of fresh
   rosemary (dried is fine too,
   if you don't have fresh),
   coarsely chopped
30 ml/1½ tablespoons extra
   virgin olive oil

2 baking sheets lined with foil

I feel I could probably healthify any baked recipe, but I stayed away from anything bread-related for a very long time. A lot of us are intimidated by its reputation for being complicated and time-consuming. I love bread and wanted to have another option to satisfy my cravings so that I didn't have to dive into mediocre bread baskets at restaurants. This was the first recipe I ever made, and it turned out perfectly. I like to make the breadsticks thick so that they're crunchy on the outside but still soft on the inside.

Put the warm water and yeast in a very large bowl and mix well until the yeast has dissolved. Stir in the agave syrup or honey – this small amount of sweetness helps feed the yeast, which is crucial in making the dough rise. Allow it to rest for 5 minutes.

Separately, sift together the flour, xanthan gum and salt, making sure the xanthan gum is well distributed.

Add the olive oil to the yeast mixture, then sift the dry ingredients into it, stirring well to avoid any lumps. Add the rosemary and make sure it is well incorporated. You should see a big ball of dough starting to form.

Dust a clean surface with flour and place the dough ball on it. Knead the dough for 10 minutes and flour your surface generously as you go along. You want to gently stretch the dough with your hands and fold it over itself, and repeat this action in different directions.

Roll the dough with a rolling pin into a rough circle about 30 cm/12 inches wide. Make sure the surface is nice and flat. Cover the dough tightly with clingfilm/plastic wrap, followed by a damp dish towel, and let it sit for about 90 minutes.

About 15 minutes before you are ready to bake the sticks, preheat the oven to 200°C (400°F) Gas 6.

Uncover the dough; it should have risen to double in height. Cut it in half, then cut each half into 4 long slices so you have 8 strips. The strips on the outer ends of the circle should be a perfect length for breadsticks, but you should cut the longer ones in half again. Roll each strip out with your hands to lengthen and thin it to your preferred size (they will expand in the oven). Gently twist the sticks and place them on the prepared baking sheets.

Place one baking sheet on the top rack and the other on the middle rack of the preheated oven and bake for 15 minutes. Swap the sheets around and bake for another 10 minutes. Allow to cool slightly before eating. Store in an airtight container for up to 2 days.

Party tartlets with hummus

Makes 12–14

2 tablespoons ground flaxseeds/
    linseeds
6 tablespoons water
170 g/1½ cups ground almonds/
    almond meal
a pinch of salt
2 tablespoons nutritional yeast
1½ teaspoons baking powder
dried oregano, to serve

Hummus filling
400-g/14-oz can of chickpeas,
    drained
freshly squeezed juice of 1 lemon
2 tablespoons tahini paste
1 tablespoon olive oil
sea salt and freshly ground black
    pepper, to taste

12 tartlet moulds

I never would have made savoury tarts if someone hadn't requested them from me once. I thought they would be way too complicated, fancy, and intimidating. When I gave them a go though, I realized they were actually super easy. I love the idea that you can put single servings of a delicious dip into these and have them as a contained and neat party snack. Think of these party tartlets as an elevated way to serve hummus and crackers.

Preheat the oven to 180°C (350°F) Gas 4.

Put the flaxseeds/linseeds and water in a small bowl. Whisk the seeds into the water with a fork until the mixture starts to feel like the consistency of a beaten egg – in fact, what you have are 2 "flax eggs" that play the same role as eggs in plant-based baking recipes. Place in the refrigerator.

Put the ground almonds/almond meal, salt, nutritional yeast and baking powder in a food processor. Blitz together. At the last minute, add the "flax egg" and blitz again but only until the "flax egg" has been well incorporated – you don't want to overmix this. You should see a ball of dough start to form. Remove the dough from the processor and divide it into 12. Press each portion into a tartlet mould so that it neatly lines the base and sides of the mould. Trim off any excess dough with a sharp knife.

Put the tartlet moulds on a baking sheet in the middle of the preheated oven and bake for about 15 minutes, until you see the edges of the tartlets start to brown. Allow the tartlet cases to cool for a few minutes, at which point they should pop right out of the moulds.

For the hummus filling
Blitz all the ingredients together in a food processor until smooth.

Fill each tartlet case with a generous tablespoon of hummus and sprinkle a little oregano over the top.

You can use storebought hummus if you don't have time to make your own.

Almond-flax crackers

Serves 8

¼ red onion
70 g/a little over ½ cup almonds
70 g/⅓ cup flaxseeds/linseeds
2 tablespoons miso paste
1 tablespoon water
1 teaspoon sea salt
1 teaspoon garlic powder
1 teaspoon ground cumin
freshly ground black pepper

*baking sheet lined with baking
parchment*

This is probably the recipe I make the most often out of all the recipes in this book – surprisingly, these crackers win over even the biggest healthy-eating sceptics. I bring them over to dinner parties as a thank you, or give them away as gifts. They make a great alternative to bread when you want something a little more nutrient-dense. Use them as dippers, top them with sliced veggies for your kid's lunchbox, or crumble them on top of a salad. Having a batch of these on hand keeps me away from the chips…

Preheat the oven to 180°C (350°F) Gas 4.

Slice the red onion very thinly and set aside.

In a food processor fitted with an "S" blade, blitz the almonds until they start to form a fine powder, remove and set aside. Now blitz the flaxseeds/linseeds in the processor until they start to form a fine powder. It's really important you don't do the almonds and seeds at the same time as they are different sizes and you will get an uneven texture; and if you overprocess them, you will get a paste rather than a fine meal, so don't blitz them for too long.

Now add the ground almonds to the ground flaxseeds/linseeds in the food processor, along with the red onion, miso paste, water, salt, garlic powder, cumin and pepper to taste. Blitz until you have a smooth paste.

Spread the cracker dough over the prepared baking sheet. Put another sheet of parchment on top and use a rolling pin or plastic ruler to apply pressure to the surface in order to get the dough smooth and even. It should be about 1 cm/½ inch thick.

Bake in the preheated oven for 16–18 minutes, until the middle is no longer soft. Allow to cool slightly, then break into pieces to serve.

Baked tortilla chips with nectarine-tomato salsa

Serves 6–8

10–12 all-corn tortillas
1 teaspoon sea salt

Nectarine-tomato salsa
1 nectarine
450 g/1 lb. cherry tomatoes
½ red onion
½ fresh jalapeño pepper (optional)
3 tablespoons freshly chopped
   coriander/cilantro
1 teaspoon chilli powder
1 lime
2 tablespoons apple cider vinegar

2 baking sheets lined with foil

Tortilla chips and salsa are THE snack you just can't stop eating once you start. And with this recipe, there's no reason why you should stop – it's one of the most delicious combos ever invented if you ask me and you can rest assured you're eating only good stuff. There aren't several teaspoons of hidden sugar in this salsa, which is plenty sweet enough from the addition of a nectarine. The tortilla chips are not fried but baked, and of course they're not dusted with a cocktail of e-numbers either. Munch and crunch to your heart's content.

Preheat the oven to 180°C (350°F) Gas 4.

Stack the tortillas on a board and cut through them into eighths to make wedges. Scatter the wedges over the prepared baking sheets and sprinkle with the salt. Bake in the preheated oven, one baking sheet at a time, for 13 minutes – don't bake both at the same time because the bottom sheet of tortillas will inevitably undercook. Thirteen minutes is really the golden number – any longer and the tortillas will become impossible to chew; any less and they won't get crunchy.

For the nectarine-tomato salsa
Dice the nectarine, cherry tomatoes, red onion and jalapeño, if using, and combine with the remaining ingredients. I don't usually find that the salsa needs much more liquid because the cherry tomatoes make it really juicy. Now put half of the mixture in a food processor, blitz until smooth, then add it to the unblended mixture. This half-blending trick makes the perfect salsa – mostly smooth and easy to scoop onto a tortilla chip, but with enough chunks for you to be able to taste all the components. Yum!

Did you know?
I recommend the half-blending technique when making chunky bean and vegetable soups, such as lentil soup. When my soup is cooked, I place half in the food processor so that the liquid part of the soup is thick and creamy.

Spicy masala kale chips

Serves 2–4

1 head of curly kale or 1 bag
   of pre-chopped curly kale
   (about 50 g/1¾ oz.)
1 large tomato, quartered
3 sun-dried tomatoes (dry
   not marinated ones, with no
   added sugar)
½ teaspoon paprika
¼ teaspoon ground cumin
a pinch of sea salt
⅛–¼ teaspoon cayenne pepper
freshly ground black pepper

baking sheet lined with foil

Kale chips have burst on the scene in a big way as a healthier alternative to processed crunchy snack foods like potato chips and popcorn. However, most commercial versions are coated with cashews, which I find makes them a lot heavier and more calorific than they could be. Cashews tend to encourage the formation of yeast in the body, so I used to tend to avoid kale chips altogether. However, kale is one of the best things you can put in your body, and turning them into chips is a brilliant way to sneak them into your diet in a fun way, so I set out to make my own version. My requirements were that they had to be moreish, but also light enough that you could eat the entire batch in front of a good film without feeling guilty, like you do with the aforementioned popcorn.

The obvious alternative to using a nut-based coating for the chips was to go for something like olive oil, which worked great with a little salt. But I wanted to find a completely fat-free version so that even those with the most stringent diets could enjoy them. I got the idea to try a tomato-based coating, and the spicy masala combination was born from there. Nowadays, you can find almost every flavour of kale chip out there, from chocolate to wasabi, but I think this one may be my favourite!

Preheat the oven to 200°C (400°F) Gas 6.

Tear small pieces of kale off the stems and place them in a colander. Wash them, then dry them as thoroughly as possible – ideally they should be completely dry. Place the dry pieces in a large bowl.

Put the tomato quarters and sun-dried tomatoes in a food processor. Pulse until smooth, scraping down the sides of the bowl as you go. It won't seem like a lot of mixture, but the idea is just to flavour the kale rather than cover it in a thick sauce. Add the paprika, cumin and salt, then as much cayenne and black pepper as you like, depending on how spicy you want your chips to turn out. Process the mixture again, then pour it into the bowl of kale. Using your hands, toss the kale so that it is evenly coated in the masala mixture.

Spread the kale pieces onto the prepared baking sheet and bake in the preheated oven with the door slightly ajar for about 14–16 minutes. You will know the kale is ready when it is totally crispy and thin. If you can resist eating it all immediately, store it in an airtight container for about 4–5 days at room temperature.

Sesame-crusted green beans

Serves 4–6

1 tablespoon ground flaxseeds/
   linseeds
3 tablespoons tamari soy sauce
1 tablespoon agave syrup
60 g/½ cup sesame seeds
1 packet of fresh green beans
   (about 2 dozen), trimmed

*baking sheet lined with baking
   parchment or foil*

When I first came up with the idea of sesame-crusted bean sticks as a fun party snack, I thought I must have unconsciously tricked myself into thinking that a well-known hors d'oeuvre was my own. It is so obvious, I thought to myself, that it must be a thing, right? I asked several people if it was already a common combination but it didn't seem to be, so I played around in the kitchen to make it. These make really elegant nibbles to serve to guests, especially if you're giving them Asian food afterwards.

Preheat the oven to 180°C (350°F) Gas 4.

If you're serving these beans as finger food, you may want to cut them in half to make them easier to eat in one bite. Otherwise, leave them whole.

Put the flaxseeds/linseeds, soy sauce and agave syrup in a wide bowl and whisk with a fork until mixture has thickened slightly. Put the sesame seeds in another wide bowl.

Place each green bean into the marinade, one at a time, then dip into the sesame seeds. Once fully coated, place on the prepared baking sheet.

Bake the beans in the preheated oven for 12 minutes – they should be softened on the outside but still crunchy on the inside.

Did you know?
We associate the nutrient beta-carotene with foods like carrots, sweet potatoes, melons and mangoes because it's what gives them their orange colour. But did you know that most green veggies are also great sources of this powerful antioxidant? The reason you can't tell is because their chlorophyll content makes them green, thereby hiding the orange colour they would otherwise give off. Green beans are a great example of this, and other examples include kale, spinach, asparagus, broccoli and chilli peppers. It's important to load up on beta-carotene because our bodies convert it to Vitamin A, which we need for immunity and fighting infection, healthy cell and mucus membrane growth, and more vainly, beautiful skin, hair and nails.

Cinema snacks,
revisited

Serves 1

Masala popcorn
1 tablespoon corn kernels
½ teaspoon sea salt
1 tablespoon chaat masala (to make
   your own, mix a pinch each of
   garam masala, ground cumin,
   ground fennel seeds, ground
   ginger, black pepper and paprika)

Fizzy lemonade
ice, to serve
500 ml/2 cups naturally sparkling
   water
freshly squeezed juice of ½ lemon
1 teaspoon xylitol or stevia

When I was a child, fizzy drinks were not a part of my vocabulary. I hardly even knew what Coca Cola was until age 11, when I went to a friend's house and they offered me every kind of soft drink on the planet. We were also allowed to watch films all day and eat copious amounts of snacks at this friend's house. Needless to say, my sister and I went over there as often as we could!

Our friend's grandmother, who lived in the same house, used to make huge bowls of popcorn for us to enjoy with our movies. Being Indian, she used to dress the popcorn with a generous shake of chaat masala, a dry mix from her spice rack, and I loved it immediately. My favourite "treat" ended up being a chaat masala popcorn with an ice-cold Sprite – the perfect combination of sweet, salty and spicy. Now, I make it the healthy way, with home-popped corn without any added fat, and no nasties from the sugary sodas.

For the masala popcorn
Put the corn kernels in a non-stick saucepan over medium heat and place the lid on top. As soon as you hear the corn start to pop, turn the heat down to low. Remove when all corn has popped – about 45–60 seconds. Toss the freshly popped corn with the salt and chaat masala and place in a big bowl. You have full permission to eat the entire serving yourself!

For the fizzy lemonade
Put some ice in a large glass and pour in the sparkling water and lemon juice. Add the sweetener and stir well.

Variations
Basil and oregano: add 1 teaspoon olive oil to the corn kernels in the pan. Pop as above, then remove from the heat and toss in 1 tablespoon each of dried basil and dried oregano.
Cheesy truffle: add 1 teaspoon truffle-infused olive oil to the corn kernels in the pan. Pop as above, then remove from the heat and toss in 3 teaspoons nutritional yeast, which will give the popcorn a slightly cheesy flavour.
Sweet treat: add 1 teaspoon coconut oil mixed with 1 teaspoon vanilla extract to the corn kernels in the pan. Pop as above, then remove from the heat and toss in a generous pinch of ground cinnamon.

NYC-style glazed nuts

Serves 6

2 tablespoons coconut oil
2 tablespoons agave syrup
  (I prefer agave in this recipe
  because it's slightly stickier
  than other liquid sweeteners)
1 teaspoon grated nutmeg
350 g/about 2½ cups mixed nuts,
  eg almonds, peanuts, cashews,
  hazelnuts, soy nuts
2 tablespoons xylitol or stevia,
  or other granulated sweetener
½ teaspoon arrowroot or
  cornflour/cornstarch
50 g/½ cup ground almonds/
  almond meal

baking sheet lined with foil

The smell of sweet glazed nuts on every corner is one of my favourite things about New York City. I love it so much that I bought a bag of them once, just to taste them so I could recreate them for myself in a healthy way. This version is pretty authentic, using ground almonds/almond meal in place of white sugar to give them that slightly gritty texture that the classic ones have too.

Preheat the oven to 200°C (400°F) Gas 6.

Put the coconut oil in a medium saucepan and heat until melted. Remove from the heat and allow it to cool for a few minutes, then stir in the agave syrup and grated nutmeg.

Add the nuts to the saucepan and toss to coat well in the liquid. Using a slotted spoon, transfer the nuts to a bowl. Reserve the remaining liquid in the pan for later.

Put the sweetener and arrowroot or cornflour/cornstarch in a high-speed blender and blitz until finely ground. Combine this with the ground almonds/almond meal, then tip into the bowl of nuts. Mix well, to coat, then transfer the nuts to the prepared baking sheet. Pour the reserved liquid over the nuts and toss them.

Roast the nuts in the preheated oven for 30 minutes, then allow to cool for 5 minutes before serving. Store in an airtight container for up to 5 days.

Bombay mix

Serves 8

3–4 tablespoons peanut oil
   (or almond oil, coconut oil or
   grapeseed oil if you don't have
   peanut oil)
70 g/½ cup yellow split peas
35 g/¼ cup cashews
35 g/¼ cup peanuts
35 g/¼ cup pumpkin seeds
110 g/2 cups plain corn flakes
   (with no added sugar)
3 tablespoons unsweetened
   flaked coconut
3–4 slices dried mango, finely
   chopped
2 tablespoons raisins
½ teaspoon ground cumin
¼ teaspoon paprika
1 teaspoon ground turmeric
½ teaspoon sea salt
½ teaspoon onion powder
2 teaspoons Worcestershire sauce
   (look for a vegan variety,
   if you prefer)
freshly squeezed juice of 1 lime
1 fresh green chilli, deseeded
   and sliced
1 tablespoon water (optional)

Who doesn't love a good, salty bar snack? It's my mother's savoury teatime treat of choice, so inevitably it used to make its way into our house all the time, and it was hard to resist. Here is a version you don't have to feel guilty about, and it won't leave you feeling sluggish afterwards.

The list of ingredients is long, but don't be put off – the whole thing takes about 10 minutes to prepare, and if you don't have some of the components, feel free to omit them.

Heat the oil in a saucepan over medium heat. Fry the split peas, cashews, peanuts and pumpkin seeds for a few minutes until the split peas have softened and are cooked through. Add the corn flakes and toss until crispy.

Add all the remaining ingredients. If the mixture gets dry, feel free to drizzle in the tablespoon of water. Stir to combine, remove from the heat and discard any remaining moisture or oil.

Allow to cool, then refrigerate in an airtight container until you're ready to serve it. It will keep for up to 1 week. If it softens after a few days, toast it slightly in the oven.

yellow split peas

peanuts

cashews

pumpkin seeds

flaked coconut

dried mango

corn flakes

Jalapeño onion rings

Makes about 3 dozen

3 tablespoons ground flaxseeds/
   linseeds
175 ml/⅔ cup water
170 g/1 cup cornmeal
150 g/1 cup gluten-free crackers,
   processed into crumbs
1 large fresh jalapeño pepper,
   thinly sliced and deseeded if
   you don't like things too spicy
½ teaspoon sea salt
freshly ground black pepper
2 large onions, cut into
   2-cm/1-inch thick slices

2 baking sheets lined with foil

To me, onion rings evoke a whimsical, 1950s American playfulness that I love, and the importance of the vibe around our food cannot be discounted. Before we even taste something, the anticipation of it influences our eventual enjoyment of it. For this reason, the fun should never be left out of food.

Preheat the oven to 220°C (425°F) Gas 7.

Mix the flaxseeds/linseeds and water and set aside. Separately, mix the cornmeal, cracker crumbs, jalapeño, salt, and pepper to taste in a wide bowl.

Separate the onion slices into rings. Dip them into the flaxseed/linseed mixture, then into the crumb mixture. For each onion ring, do this twice so that they are double-coated.

Arrange the rings on the prepared baking sheets and bake in the preheated oven for 8–12 minutes until they are slightly browned on the outside and cooked all the way through. Serve with Healthified Ketchup (below).

Healthified ketchup

Makes about 1 cupful

250 ml/1 cup plain tomato passata/
   strained tomatoes
1 teaspoon celery salt or Herbamare
½ teaspoon garlic powder
1 teaspoon onion powder
1 tablespoon xylitol
1 tablespoon apple cider vinegar
4 teaspoons cornflour/cornstarch
2 tablespoons water

I was one of those kids who loved ketchup with everything – with plain pasta, bread and butter, and every vegetable that was put in front of me. Now that I am older and know a little better, I realize that ketchup addiction is one big sugar rush in disguise. I still love the flavours though, and it turns out, it's super simple to make your own! I now keep a batch of this in my fridge to eat with grilled courgettes/zucchini, sautéed mushrooms, veggie burgers, corn and of course, Jalapeño Onion Rings (above).

Put the passata, celery salt, garlic powder, onion powder, xylitol and vinegar in a saucepan over medium heat. Heat gently for about 15 minutes without letting it boil. Separately, put the cornflour/cornstarch and water in a small bowl or cup, and stir until combined.

Taste the tomato mixture in the pan and add more salt or xylitol to taste. Remove from the stove, and stir in the cornflour/cornstarch mixture. As you stir, it will start to thicken until you get that more authentic ketchup texture. Store in an airtight container in the fridge for up to 1 week.

Zucchini UN-fries

Serves 3–4

80 ml/⅓ cup almond milk
35 g/¼ cup quinoa flour
35 g/¼ cup ground flaxseeds/
    linseeds
1 teaspoon garlic powder
½ teaspoon onion powder
½ teaspoon freshly ground
    black pepper
½ teaspoon sea salt
2 large courgettes/zucchini,
    cut into 5-mm/¼-inch slices

*baking sheet lined with baking
    parchment*

I don't know anyone who doesn't have a weakness for the fried courgette/zucchini side dish that most Italian restaurants offer. I don't generally like the taste of fried foods, but once you have one of these, you can't stop eating them. This version is baked instead, and the health benefits have been boosted by the addition of Omega-3s in the form of ground flaxseeds/linseeds. Eat these as a snack like I do, or serve them alongside your healthy dinner.

If you wanted a spicier version, you could substitute the onion powder and black pepper for some cayenne pepper.

Preheat the oven to 220°C (425°F) Gas 7.

Put the almond milk in a bowl and set aside. Put all the remaining ingredients (except the courgettes/zucchini) in a separate, wide bowl and mix well.

Place each slice of courgette/zucchini into the almond milk, one at a time, then dip into the dry mixture. Once fully coated, place on the prepared baking sheet.

Bake the UN-fries in the preheated oven for 15 minutes. Remove from the oven, flip the slices over, and bake for another 15 minutes. Keep a close eye on them, as they burn easily. They can be served warm from the oven or at room temperature. Store in an airtight container for up to 3 days.

Creole cauliflower

Serves 3–4

1 large head of cauliflower, cut into
    florets about 1 cm/½ inch thick
2 tablespoons black treacle/
    molasses or maple syrup
4–5 tablespoons tomato passata/
    strained tomatoes (or
    1 tablespoon tomato paste mixed
    with 4 tablespoons water if you
    don't have passata on hand)
1 teaspoon cayenne pepper
2 teaspoons paprika
1 teaspoon ground cumin
½ teaspoon dried thyme
½ teaspoon garlic powder
1 teaspoon sea salt
freshly ground black pepper

*baking sheet lined with baking
    parchment*

About a year ago, "cauliflower popcorn" started popping up in raw food circles. The idea was that you could dehydrate tiny pieces of cauliflower until crunchy, like popcorn. I tried it a few times with salt and/or nutritional yeast but I felt it could do with a little more zing. That's when I got the idea to flavour it with Creole rub, which my friend Cleo introduced me to. Creole rub is a mix of southern American flavours normally used to flavour meat with. You do have to make this ahead of time, as it takes about 6 hours in the oven or dehydrator.

Preheat the oven to 115°C (225°F) Gas ¼, with the fan on if possible.

Wash the cauliflower florets thoroughly, then place in a large bowl. Put all the remaining ingredients in a separate, wide bowl and mix well.

Pour the mixture over the cauliflower in the bowl and toss until well coated.

Scatter the cauliflower on a baking sheet and bake in the preheated oven for about 6 hours, until thoroughly dried and crisp.

Dips & Dippers

When hunger strikes and you're tempted to reach for that tub of cheese dip and those breadsticks, stop! Once you see the myriad colours, textures and flavour combinations to be enjoyed with your own homemade dips and dippers, you'll never look back. You can be so creative with fresh fruit and vegetables to turn them into vibrant dips and amazingly nutritious alternatives to bread, breadsticks, crackers and chips. Turn the pages of this chapter and discover super guacamole, lettuce wraps with sweet chilli sauce and fabulous quinoa sushi wraps for dipping into soy sauce.

Mango-avocado summer rolls with lime dipping sauce

Makes 6

6 rice paper wrappers
1 soft avocado, stoned and cut
    into slivers
2 mangoes, stoned and cut
    into slivers
small handful of alfalfa sprouts
3 large tablespoons of coriander/
    cilantro leaves
handful of pea shoots
handful of mixed salad leaves
    (I used watercress)
small handful of cashews (optional)
1 lime

Lime dipping sauce
1 lime
2–3 tablespoons tamari soy sauce
1 tablespoon balsamic vinegar

I could eat Asian food every day for the rest of my life. I could also eat avocado every day (which I already do). Back when I was first learning to cut gluten from my diet, I was introduced to making spring rolls the Vietnamese way, rolling them in rice paper rather than frying them up, and I haven't looked back since.

Along with the creamy avocado and sweet mango, these rolls are packed with my three favourite ingredients for nutritional value: watercress, coriander/cilantro and alfalfa sprouts. Watercress is up there with kale, boasting a perfect score of 1000 on the ANDI scale (Aggregate Nutrient Density Index). I consume coriander/cilantro daily as it's one of the few foods that helps chelate heavy metals out of the body (such as mercury, lead and aluminium, which we accumulate through pollution, water, and everyday products). And sprouts should be regarded a food group all of their own because they contain up to 100 times the enzymes that regular fruits and veggies do, as well as several times the protein and vitamin content.

Fill a large bowl with warm water and place a rice paper wrapper in the bowl to soak and soften for about 1 minute. Soak the sheets one by one, otherwise they will stick together as they soften.

Remove the rice paper from the bowl and place it onto a dish towel to soak up the excess water. (Meanwhile, put a second wrapper in the bowl of warm water to soften.) Spoon one-sixth of the avocado, mango, sprouts, coriander/cilantro, pea shoots, salad leaves and cashews, if using, onto one half of the sheet in a neat column. Squeeze some lime juice over the filling. Fold the sides of the sheet up onto the filling, then tightly roll up the sheet over the filling to make a compact roll. Set aside and repeat this whole process with the remaining rice paper wrappers and filling.

For the lime dipping sauce
In a small dish, mix together the lime juice, soy sauce and balsamic vinegar.

To serve, cut each roll in half on the diagonal and dip into a little bowl of the lime dipping sauce.

Black bean dip

Makes I cupful

2 teaspoons extra virgin olive oil
¼ onion, diced
I tomato, diced
400-g/14-oz. can of black beans,
   rinsed
2 teaspoons of freshly chopped
   coriander/cilantro
I teaspoon ground cumin
a pinch of sea salt
a pinch of freshly ground
   black pepper
½ teaspoon chilli powder (optional)
freshly squeezed juice of I lime
2 spring onions/scallions, chopped

I've tasted a lot of bland black bean dips in my lifetime. Often, restaurants rely on topping them with sour cream to make them a little tastier. Black beans are particularly high in antioxidants and a great source of fibre and protein, so they deserve another chance! This version is different in that it uses sautéed rather than raw onions and tomatoes, and this makes the end result so savoury and moreish. Just the thought of this dip now makes my mouth water! Dip some bell pepper strips, cauliflower florets or Baked Tortilla Chips (page 62) into it for a rounded snack. For a Mexican-themed meal, serve it with salsa, avocado and a gluten-free grain such as quinoa, brown rice or millet. You can also spread it on a wholegrain wrap and top it with fillings of your choice.

Heat I teaspoon of the olive oil in a saucepan over medium heat. Fry the onion and tomato until soft and the onions have browned, then allow to cool for a few minutes.

Transfer the onion and tomato to a food processor and add the black beans, coriander/cilantro, cumin, salt, pepper and chilli powder, if using. Pulse until mostly smooth, to your preference – you may want it a little on the chunky side. Garnish with the remaining olive oil and the spring onions/scallions.

Garlic and white bean dip

Makes I cupful

2 garlic cloves, skin on
400-g/14-oz. can of white beans,
   eg butter beans
I tablespoon freshly squeezed
   lemon juice
½ teaspoon sea salt
I teaspoon dried oregano
½ teaspoon dried rosemary
4 tablespoons extra virgin olive oil

I love to spread this dip onto thick, crusty bread as a substitute for butter. It's lighter in calories, cholesterol-free, and has a much more complex flavour. For a complete meal, you can also mix a big dollop onto steamed spinach and quinoa, or stuff a baked sweet potato with it, along with a rocket/arugula salad. And of course, it's always easy to serve with crudités as a healthy snack.

Preheat the grill/broiler to medium.

Put the garlic cloves on a baking sheet and grill/broil for 2–3 minutes until they have roasted. Watch them closely as they burn easily.

Remove the skins from the garlic cloves and put the garlic in a food processor with the white beans, lemon juice, salt, oregano, rosemary and 3 tablespoons of the olive oil. Blitz until smooth, then pour the remaining olive oil on top.

Zesty almond pesto

Makes I cupful

20 g/1 cup each spinach, fresh mint,
    parsley and coriander/cilantro,
    tightly packed
30 g/¼ cup blanched almonds
6 tablespoons extra virgin olive oil,
    plus extra to preserve
1 kaffir lime leaf
freshly squeezed juice of 1 lime
grated zest of 1 lemon
1 garlic clove
a pinch of sea salt

Traditionally, pesto is made with basil, pine nuts and Parmesan.
I love this cheese-free version made with a mixture of herbs and
almonds in place of the pine nuts. The zingy flavours from the
kaffir lime leaf and the lemon zest make it taste more Asian than
Italian. If you can't find kaffir lime, use lemongrass as a substitute.

Use this pesto as a marinade for fish or tofu, mix into some
warm noodles with bok choy, or flavour a stir-fry of green
vegetables with it.

Put all the ingredients in a food processor and blitz until they turn into a
paste. Store in an airtight container in the fridge for up to 4 days. Pour more
olive oil onto the pesto to preserve its bright green colour, if you like.

Lighter guacamole

Makes I cupful

1 large avocado, stoned
90 g/1½ cups peas, ideally fresh,
    but frozen and thawed is fine too
½ red (bell) pepper, deseeded
2 tomatoes
¼ small onion
1 garlic clove
large handful of fresh coriander/
    cilantro
freshly squeezed juice of ½ lime
1 tablespoon freshly squeezed
    lemon juice, plus extra
    to preserve

Although traditional guacamole is made with all-healthful
ingredients, we are often advised to exercise portion control when
eating it due to the high fat and calorie content. It's ironic then,
that it's one of those foods that's so easy to dig into and finish the
whole bowl before you've even realized it. This version has been
lightened up by including a hefty dose of fresh peas and extra
veggies, which allow the guacamole to keep its creamy texture
and body, but which mellow out the density of the avocado.

Put all the ingredients in a food processor and blitz until smooth. Serve
immediately or if keeping in the fridge, squeeze more lemon juice onto
the surface of the dip to prevent the avocado from browning.

Chard and cabbage wraps with peanut sauce

Makes 4 large wraps

4 large chard leaves (regular chard
    or rainbow chard, which has a
    red or orange stem)
½ head of white or red cabbage,
    or ¼ of each, finely chopped
2 carrots, grated
1 orange, halved
4 tablespoons sunflower seeds
1 tablespoon tamari soy sauce

Peanut sauce
4 tablespoons peanut butter
1 garlic clove, crushed
1 teaspoon grated ginger (or you
    can use ground ginger in a pinch)
2 tablespoons sesame oil
2 tablespoons red wine vinegar
freshly squeezed juice of 1 lime
½–1 teaspoon chilli powder
    (optional)

Eschew refined wheat and wrap your lunch in slightly-sweet and nutrient-dense chard instead. Try the filling here, or use Lighter Guacamole (page 84) or Nectarine-tomato Salsa (page 62).

Wash the chard and dry thoroughly with some kitchen paper/paper towels. Place each leaf face down on a board. If you can, carefully shave off the part of the stem that runs up the middle of the leaf and make small incisions along it – this will make the leaf easier to bend and roll.

Put the cabbage and carrots in a large bowl. Cut 1 orange half into small sections, and squeeze the juice from the remaining half into the bowl. Add the orange sections too.

Put the sunflower seeds in a non-stick frying pan over medium heat and toss occasionally. Dry-fry until they have browned slightly. This step is not crucial if you're in a hurry, but it does give the wraps the most unique flavour.

Add the sunflower seeds and soy sauce to the bowl and stir well.

Place a quarter of the filling at one end of a chard leaf. Cut off the white stem if it is too long. Fold the sides of the leaf up onto the filling, then roll up the leaf over the filling to make a roll.

For the peanut sauce
Put all the ingredients in a small dish and stir with a fork.

To serve, cut each roll in half on the diagonal and either dip them into the peanut sauce, or drizzle the sauce into the mouth of the wraps with a spoon.

Edamame and miso dip

Makes I cupful

200 g/1½ cups shelled edamame
   beans (fresh, or frozen and
   thawed)
I tablespoon water
3 tablespoons sweet white
   miso paste
I tablespoon extra virgin olive oil
I tablespoon tamari soy sauce
I teaspoon wasabi paste

Like the rest of the nation, I love hummus. The only problem with consuming it every day is that it doesn't help you vary your nutrients very much. So I tried to play on variations of a bean-based spread, using edamame (soy) beans, which are so underrated in my opinion. They are full of calcium and are a rare plant source of Omega-3 fatty acids.

This dip is a fun way to consume them. Eat it with cut veggies or in a sandwich with avocado, cucumber, carrots and ginger.

Put nearly all the edamame beans (reserving some for decoration) and the water in a food processor and blitz until smooth. Add the remaining ingredients and mix well so that everything is well incorporated.

Decorate with the reserved edamame beans. Store in an airtight container in the fridge for up to 5 days.

Zucchini hummus

Makes I cupful

2 courgettes/zucchini
80 ml/⅓ cup tahini paste
2–3 ice cubes
I garlic clove
freshly squeezed juice of ½ lemon,
   plus extra to preserve
a pinch of sea salt
I teaspoon smoked paprika
I tablespoon extra virgin olive oil

food processor able to crush ice cubes

I was telling a friend about my hummus addiction one day and she said she'd heard of people lightening it up by using courgettes/zucchini instead of chickpeas. It didn't sound great to me, but it turned out pretty darn good! If you're a purist, this may not satisfy you in the same way, but it's a really nice way to change things slightly. Because it's also completely bean free, it makes a great alternative for those who have trouble digesting them.

I learned about the trick of adding ice cubes from a professional hummus maker, who told me that they do this to add to the texture of fresh hummus.

If you want the colour of your dip to resemble traditional hummus, peel the courgettes/zucchini. If not, keep the skins on for added vitamins and minerals.

Roughly chop the courgettes/zucchini and put in a food processor with the tahini, ice cubes, garlic clove, lemon juice, salt and half of the paprika. Pulse until completely smooth.

Garnish with the rest of the paprika and the olive oil. Squeeze lemon juice over the top to prevent it from browning and store in an airtight container in the fridge for up to 5 days.

Eggplant and zucchini roll-ups

Makes 12–14

2 large courgettes/zucchini
1 large aubergine/eggplant
4 teaspoons extra virgin olive oil
1 teaspoon dried thyme
75 g/¾ cup pine nuts
80 ml/⅓ cup water
2 tablespoons nutritional yeast
1 tablespoon tomato paste
5–6 sun-dried tomatoes
1 tablespoon dried rosemary
1 teaspoon dried marjoram
½ teaspoon sea salt
freshly ground black pepper
handful of fresh basil leaves
3–4 tablespoons shelled
  hemp seeds

baking sheet lined with foil
cocktail sticks/toothpicks (optional)

These tasty, herb–rich roll–ups are one of the best ways to satisfy that craving for Italian food, without having to compromise your healthy intentions.

Preheat the grill/broiler to medium.

Cut the courgettes/zucchini and aubergine/eggplant lengthways into long strips about 1 cm/½ inch thick. Arrange them on the prepared baking sheets and lightly brush the aubergine/eggplant with 1 teaspoon of the olive oil. Scatter the thyme over the vegetables. Grill/broil for about 3 minutes, then flip them over and grill/broil for another 3 minutes. Watch them carefully so that they don't burn. You may have to remove the courgettes/zucchini at this point and leave the aubergine/eggplant in for another 1–2 minutes. Once done, set them aside to cool.

Put the remaining olive oil, pine nuts, water, nutritional yeast, tomato paste, sun-dried tomatoes, rosemary, marjoram and salt in a food processor and blitz until very smooth.

Take one vegetable strip, gently spread a thin layer of the mixture over it, lay some basil leaves on top and sprinkle with hemp seeds. Roll up the strip and spear with a cocktail stick/toothpick, if necessary, to seal it closed.

Did you know?

I don't like to throw around the word "superfood" because it puts us in the mindset that some healthy foods are better than others. In reality, super-health is achieved when we feast on all of nature's bounty. The humble cucumber should not be overlooked in favour of stuffing our cupboards with baobab, because the truth is that what we know about the nutrients in our food is only the tip of the iceberg. Food science is largely a new field and we have no idea of the way compounds really behave in our bodies.

Nevertheless, people are always asking me to recommend some amazing foods that they can add to their diets, and I almost always say hemp seeds. They are a rich plant source of Omega-3 fatty acids, which our society is chronically deprived of, and also a significant source of iron, magnesium and protein (an amazing 11 grams in 2 tablespoons). Their soft but crunchy texture is also strangely addictive. I sprinkle these on salads, soups or quinoa three to four times per week. Surefire signs that you are short on Omega-3s are waxy ears, joint pain and brittle hair and/or nails.

Healthy babaganoush

Serves 4–6

500–600 g/1–1½ lbs. aubergine/
   eggplant
2–3 garlic cloves
60 ml/¼ cup light tahini paste
   (light tahini is best, but regular
   is fine too if you can't find it)
½ teaspoon ground cumin
¾ teaspoon sea salt
4–5 tablespoons freshly squeezed
   lemon juice
drizzle of extra virgin olive oil
sprig of fresh flat-leaf parsley,
   to serve
handful of pomegranate seeds,
   to serve

baking sheet lined with foil

I always say that Lebanese food would be my last meal on earth. It's that one meal, composed of so many craveable sharing dishes, that I am totally unable to exercise portion control over. Inevitably, a major food coma ensues after I've been out to a Lebanese restaurant.

I decided to make a lighter version of babaganoush at home one day when I had a craving but couldn't face feeling heavy and sluggish after my dinner. Most restaurant babaganoushes are very high in fat because restaurants are heavy-handed with the tastes we are hard-wired to get addicted to. This version uses a much kinder amount of light tahini, and just a touch of olive oil.

Serve this with a salad of cucumber, tomato, red onion, parsley and lemon juice for a quick and easy meal, or use it as dip: I love it with the Rosemary Breadsticks on page 56.

Preheat the grill/broiler to medium.

Spear the skins of your aubergine/eggplant with a fork at regular intervals – this will allow any moisture to seep out. Place them on the prepared baking sheet and grill/broil them until the skins burn, about 18–20 minutes. Don't be worried if these look overdone! Leave the grill/broiler on.

Allow the aubergine/eggplant to cool slightly, then run them under cold water and you should be able to peel the skins right off. Discard the skins and place the flesh in a bowl. Cut it into smaller pieces with a knife and fork and remove any remaining moisture using a sheet of kitchen paper/paper towel.

Put the (peeled) garlic cloves on a baking sheet and grill/broil them for 2–3 minutes until they have roasted. Watch them closely as they burn easily. Crush them into the bowl with the aubergine/eggplant. Add the tahini, cumin and salt, and mix well. Refrigerate until you are ready to serve – this is important as it allows the mixture to firm up.

Five minutes before serving, put the mixture in the food processor with the lemon juice and pulse until smooth, with a few chunky bits remaining. Transfer to a serving bowl and drizzle with some olive oil. Serve with a sprig of parsley and scatter the pomegranate seeds on top.

Baby Gem lettuce wraps
with sweet chilli sauce

Makes 10–12

2 heads of Baby Gem lettuce
handful of fresh coriander/cilantro
2–3 spring onions/scallions
2 large carrots
1 pomegranate

Sweet chilli sauce
1–2 fresh chillies, to taste
  (2 chillies will be very spicy)
1 garlic clove, crushed
½ teaspoon onion powder
125 ml/½ cup rice vinegar
125 ml/½ cup water
2 big teaspoons stevia
½ teaspoon sea salt
1 tablespoon cornflour/cornstarch
2 tablespoons water

coffee grinder or spice grinder
  (optional)

On most days, lunch for me is a large salad because it makes me feel light and energized for the afternoon ahead. However, it can get boring to eat a bowl's worth of fresh veggies in the same bowl, with the same knife and fork day in, day out. I was prepping some Baby Gem hearts for a salad one day, and thought why not use them as wraps and put the salad ingredients inside. Don't just eat these for lunch – they also make a great appetizer for an informal party or dinner party.

Tear the larger, outside leaves off the Baby Gem lettuce – these will become your "wraps". Wash thoroughly and arrange on a plate.

To assemble the filling, cut the remaining lettuce as finely as you can so that it almost takes on a shredded texture. Do the same with the coriander/cilantro and spring onions/scallions, and place all three in a large bowl. Using a vegetable peeler, peel the carrots into ribbons and add to the bowl.

For the pomegranate, the best way to remove the seeds (or "arils", to use their technical name) is to cut the fruit in half and place it in a large bowl of cold water. Then tear the flesh and separate the seeds by hand. You'll see that the seeds sink to the bottom of the bowl, whereas the white flesh floats. Next, pour away the water and flesh so that you just have the seeds left.

Add the seeds to the bowl of vegetables and mix well. Using a small spoon, fill the lettuce wraps with the mixture, making sure they're not too full to hold together.

For the sweet chilli sauce
Using a coffee or spice grinder, grind the chillies to a paste. If you don't have one of these, slice the chillies as thinly as possible. For a spicy sauce, include the seeds, otherwise omit them. Put the chillies, garlic, onion powder, rice vinegar, the 125 ml/½ cup water, the stevia and salt in a saucepan over medium heat and bring to the boil. Allow the mixture to simmer until it has reduced down – 8–10 minutes.

Meanwhile, put the cornflour/cornstarch and the 2 tablespoons water in a small bowl or cup, and stir until combined. Turn the chilli mixture down to low heat and add the cornflour/cornstarch mixture. Stir slowly for a couple of minutes until the sauce has thickened.

To serve, eat the lettuce wraps by hand, dipping them into the sweet chilli sauce as you go!

Quinoa maki

Makes 8

80 g/³⁄₄ cup cooked quinoa
2 teaspoons rice vinegar
4 sheets of sushi nori, about
    20 x 20 cm/8 x 8 inches
2 carrots
10-cm/4-inch piece of cucumber
½ avocado
2–3 spring onions/scallions
handful of beansprouts
handful of microgreens, such as
    mizuna, pea shoots, or
    watercress (optional)
1 teaspoon black or white
    sesame seeds
3 tablespoons tamari soy sauce
wasabi, to serve (optional)
pickled ginger, to serve (optional)

Sushi is well known as a healthy choice. Collectively though, we have never been more aware of what's healthy and what isn't – to the point where I feel Japanese restaurants are missing a trick by only offering traditional sushi rolls, made with white sushi rice (usually prepared with white sugar). Until the day we can get a healthier fix for sushi and sushi rolls on the high street, here are some quinoa maki to satisfy that craving.

This is a great way to use up quinoa or other grain leftovers from last night's dinner.

Put the quinoa and rice vinegar in a bowl and toss to coat.

Cut the nori sheets in half diagonally so that you have 8 triangular pieces. Cut the carrots and cucumber into matchsticks. Cut the avocado in half and make fine slices into the flesh, then peel off the skin. Chop the spring onions/scallions.

Take one nori triangle and spoon 1 tablespoon of the quinoa in a line along one of the short sides of the triangle. Place a few carrot and cucumber matchsticks on top, 2 or 3 slices of the avocado, a few beansprouts and microgreens, if using, and some spring onions/scallions. Try to put a greater portion of the vegetables towards what will be the larger end of your sushi cone. Roll the nori up all around the filling, then scatter a few sesame seeds at the mouth of the cone. Repeat with the rest of the nori pieces.

Serve with soy sauce, wasabi and pickled ginger, if using.

Did you know?
In macrobiotic cuisine, seaweeds are a food group all of their own. They are so full of nutrients because these help the seaweed absorb what little sunlight reaches them so that they can grow. Aside from using this sushi nori to wrap sushi with, you can also use seaweeds in soups, crumbled dry over salads, or – my favourite – mixed into warm grain and bean dishes. Some seaweeds to try include arame, wakame, dulse and kombu.

Sweet Bites

We all get cravings for something sweet, in particular for chocolate. But when people make the decision to cut down on sugar, wheat and/or dairy, they assume they will have to wave goodbye to those all-time favourite treats. But that's not the case! Good-quality dark chocolate, coconut sugar, dried fruit, nuts and corn flakes, for example, along with some clever techniques, will get you all the way to sweet nirvana, without any of the guilt and dentists' visits along the way. There's even an ingenious way to recreate decadent ice cream without any of the naughtiness!

Almond butter cups

Makes 12 large cups,
or 24 mini cups

215 ml/1 cup coconut oil
60 g/¾ cup unsweetened
  cocoa powder
4 tablespoons agave syrup
1 tablespoon stevia (or 2 more
  tablespoons agave syrup)
dash of vanilla extract
4–5 tablespoons almond butter,
  storebought or homemade
  (page 51)
1 teaspoon nutritional yeast
a pinch of salt (if using unsalted
  almond butter)

*12-hole muffin pan, or 24-hole
mini muffin pan, lined with
(eco-friendly) paper cases*

This is a spin on the classic American confectionery, Peanut Butter Cups. Don't get me wrong, I LOVE the combination of peanut butter and chocolate. But since I prefer the taste of almond butter, I once subbed it for the peanut butter in this recipe and found it even tastier. As an added bonus, almonds are rich in Vitamin E and contain less saturated fat than peanuts.

I've used nutritional yeast in this recipe, which is a dried inactive yeast that gives the almond butter an amazing flavour kick. Much like brewer's yeast, nutritional yeast contains the complete profile of B vitamins, as well as being composed of 50% protein. You can of course leave this out if you choose, but it really does take things up a notch!

Put the coconut oil in a saucepan over low heat and allow to melt. Stir in the cocoa powder, agave syrup, stevia, if using, and vanilla extract until you have smooth liquid chocolate. Divide one third of the mixture between the muffin cases and put the whole muffin pan in the freezer until the mixture has solidified – about 5 minutes.

Meanwhile, mix the almond butter, nutritional yeast and salt, if needed, in a bowl.

Remove the muffin pan from the freezer and place a generous teaspoon of the almond-yeast mixture in the centre of each base of frozen chocolate, then flatten it slightly with your fingers. Pour the remaining melted chocolate over the almond-yeast mixture. Put the whole muffin pan in the freezer again until the mixture has solidified – about 10 minutes.

Remove the almond butter cups from the freezer just before serving to get them at their most firm and crisp. If you store them in the freezer or fridge, they will keep for 3–4 weeks (unless you devour them before!)

Banana soft serve

This is not a recipe really; it's more of a clever trick that raw foodists use when they want ice cream. It seems so ridiculously simple, that I wondered why I hadn't tried it before. You will need a high-speed blender strong enough to break down frozen fruit until smooth and creamy.

For the basic recipe, you will need 2 large bananas. Peel them, cut them in half and place in a sandwich bag to freeze for at least 3 hours. It's crucial that the bananas are frozen straight through, otherwise you won't get an authentic ice-creamy texture. Put the frozen bananas plus any chosen flavourings (see below) in a food processor and blitz until smooth. Make sure you hold on to your food processor when it's running at first, as it will shake! The soft serve will be done when it's completely smooth but still thick. The trick is in the timing: stop the food processor as soon as there are no more banana "bits" in there, but don't leave it on too long, otherwise you'll have more of a melty smoothie than a soft serve.

Variations

Vanilla or maca: add a dash of vanilla extract or ½ teaspoon of maca powder, which is a sweet, caramel-y superfood from Peru. Maca is a root vegetable among a small group of foods called adaptogens; these are foods that work with our adrenal systems to help us naturally balance our hormone levels from within. Maca is an ideal natural supplement if you live a high-stress lifestyle, suffer from PCOS and other hormonal imbalances, or want to increase stamina.

Chocolate: add a generous tablespoon of unsweetened cocoa powder.

Strawberry: add 4 chopped strawberries, fresh or frozen. Using frozen fruit will help the soft serve keep its thick texture, so it's preferable to go with frozen if possible.

Some other ideas: add a small handful of frozen mango or blueberries; or 1 generous teaspoon of ground cinnamon and/or grated nutmeg; or 1 serving of espresso powder. Get creative by using anything in frozen or powdered form.

Banana split: make 1 portion of strawberry soft serve and spoon it between 2 banana halves, then top with some of the Coconut Whip (page 27) and sprinkle some berries or chocolate chips on top. Mmm!

Did you know?

The trick to eating fruit properly is to always consume it on an empty stomach so that there are no other foods blocking its quick elimination. Eat fruit either 3 hours after a meal or first thing in the morning – and yes, that means you are absolutely allowed to eat Banana Soft Serve for breakfast, without any guilt!

Strawberry

Maca

Chocolate

Frozen cookie dough balls

Makes 18–24

60 g/⅓ cup xylitol
75 g/⅓ cup non-hydrogenated
   sunflower spread, at room
   temperature
about 120 g/¾ cup brown
   gluten-free plain/all-purpose
   flour of choice
1½ teaspoons vanilla extract
½ teaspoon salt
175 g/1 cup dark/bittersweet
   chocolate chips, or coarsely
   chopped dark/bittersweet
   chocolate

freezer-proof baking sheet or plate,
lined with clingfilm/plastic wrap

When I was 12 years old, my family and I spent three months in the States. By then I had already established a sweet tooth and I discovered cookie dough, the storebought sweet logs that you could either eat straight up or shape into cookies and cook. I would scoop it straight out of the packaging and eat bowls-full in front of the TV every night, with ice cream. It was far from healthy but I never forgot how good it was. Fast forward to a couple of years ago when I made my first batch of vegan chocolate chip cookies and taste-tested the dough. I was suddenly flooded with memories of my favourite American treat, and rolled a few balls of cookie dough to keep in the freezer for later. It turns out, they tasted even better really cold, and I've continued making them like this ever since. I now omit the baking powder from my original recipe since these babies don't go anywhere near an oven!

Put the xylitol in a high-speed blender and blend until you a have a powdery, icing/confectioners' sugar-like substance.

Put the sunflower spread in a large bowl and mash with a fork. Add the flour and powdered xylitol and whisk slowly with a handheld electric whisk. With dry powders you want to make sure you're gentle to start with or they'll fly all over the place. Add the vanilla extract and salt once the mixture is smooth and whisk them in.

Finally, add the chocolate chips and stir to combine.

Pull off bite-size pieces of the dough with your fingers and roll them into neat balls. Lay them out on the prepared baking sheet and freeze for at least 30 minutes. Once they've frozen, you can transfer them to a freezer bag. Consume frozen.

Chocolate-covered caramels

Makes about 6

200 g/1 cup dates, stoned
1 tablespoon smooth peanut butter
(look for unsweetened, made
without any hydrogenated oils)
1 tablespoon coconut oil
a pinch of salt
250 g/9 oz. dark/bittersweet
chocolate (preferably sweetened
with unrefined sugar, or
unsweetened if you can't
have sugar), chopped

*freezer-proof baking sheet or plate,
lined with clingfilm/plastic wrap*

Storebought caramel: you are delicious. I used to love you.
But you are made with white sugar boiled in water and then
mixed with cream or butter, along with a host of additives and
preservatives. So I'll make my own, even more delicious version
of you with vitamin-rich dates and a touch of peanut butter.

Put the dates in a bowl of room-temperature water and allow them to soak
for a few hours. They will soften and absorb some of the water, which will
help when making the caramel.

Rinse the dates and put them in a food processor. Blitz until smooth, scraping
down the edges of the bowl as you go. Once the dates have started to form
a paste, add the peanut butter and continue to pulse. Lastly, add the coconut
oil for texture and the salt to bring out the flavour.

Process again until the mixture naturally forms a large ball.

Pull off bite-size pieces of the mixture with your fingers and roll them into
neat balls. Lay them out on the prepared baking sheet and freeze for at
least 30 minutes.

Meanwhile, put the chocolate in a heatproof bowl over a saucepan of
barely simmering water. Do not let the base of the bowl touch the water.
Leave until melted and completely smooth.

Remove the chilled caramel balls from the freezer. Place 1 caramel on
a spoon and dip it into the melted chocolate so that it is completely and
evenly coated. Return the ball to the prepared baking sheet. You can use
2 teaspoons to help shape the chocolate coating if that helps. Repeat with
the remaining caramel balls, then freeze for at least 20 minutes to give the
chocolate and caramel layers enough time to harden properly. Once they've
frozen, you can transfer them to a freezer bag.

Remove the caramels from the freezer just before serving. Store them in
the freezer for up to 2 weeks.

Walnut-goji Nanaimo bars

Makes about 16

Bottom layer
1 tablespoon ground flaxseeds/
  linseeds
3 tablespoons water
110 g/½ cup non-hydrogenated
  sunflower spread
110 g/2 cups plain corn flakes,
  with no added sugar
30 g/⅓ cup unsweetened
  cocoa powder
less than 45 g/¼ cup xylitol
75 g/1 cup unsweetened
  desiccated coconut

Middle layer
110 g/½ cup non-hydrogenated
  sunflower spread
300 g/2 cups coconut sugar
  (or other granulated sweetener,
  but coconut sugar really gives it
  a caramel-y flavour that works
  so well here)
2 teaspoons xanthan gum
1 tablespoon arrowroot
1 tablespoon maca powder (this
  will give a caramel-y flavour but
  if you don't have it, substitute
  with gluten-free plain/all-purpose
  flour of choice)
large handful of goji berries
½ teaspoon vanilla extract
2 tablespoons cherry juice or
  lemon juice, for tartness

Top layer
175 g/1 cup dark/bittersweet
  chocolate chips, or coarsely
  chopped dark/bittersweet
  chocolate
180 ml/¾ cup almond milk
handful of walnuts, chopped

*20- or 23-cm/8- or 9-inch square
  baking pan, lined with baking
  parchment*

Nanaimo bars are three-layer bars named after the town in Canada where they originated. If you stick closely to the original recipe, you make the middle layer with custard or custard powder, but here we're using vegan substitutes with the addition of goji berries whipped into the mixture, which surprisingly give it an authentic butterscotch taste. Traditional Nanaimo bars also have nuts ground into the base layer but I find that makes them too heavy, so I use ground corn flakes instead, and press a few walnuts into the top layer, so you don't lose the nuttiness altogether.

For the bottom layer
Put the flaxseeds/linseeds and water in a small bowl. Whisk the seeds into the water with a fork until the mixture starts to feel like the consistency of a beaten egg – in fact, what you have is a "flax egg" that plays the same role as an egg in plant-based baking recipes. Place in the refrigerator.

Meanwhile, put the sunflower spread in a heatproof bowl over a saucepan of barely simmering water and allow to melt. Put the corn flakes in a food processor and pulse until they have formed a coarse meal – it should be crunchy without any obvious corn-flake pieces. Once the sunflower spread has melted, stir in the cocoa powder and xylitol. Remove from the heat and stir in the ground corn flakes, desiccated coconut and "flax egg". Tip into the prepared baking pan and press it down. Use the back of a big spoon to smooth it level. Refrigerate while you prepare the middle layer.

For the middle layer
Cream together the sunflower spread and coconut sugar with a handheld electric whisk until pale. Add the xanthan gum, arrowroot and maca powder and whisk again – the mixture will start to thicken up. Stir in the goji berries, vanilla extract and juice. Remove the pan from the freezer and spread this middle layer evenly over the bottom layer. Freeze again.

For the top layer
Put the chocolate and almond milk in a heatproof bowl over a saucepan of barely simmering water. Leave until melted and completely smooth.

Remove the pan from the freezer and spread the melted chocolate mixture on top. Press the walnuts into the surface of the chocolate. Freeze again until totally hardened – about 45 minutes.

To serve, cut into 5-cm/2-inch squares and serve cold.

NB don't worry if the middle layer starts to separate slightly, it's natural when using unhydrogenated fats.

No-bake crispie cakes

Makes 24

100 g/3½ oz. dark/bittersweet
  chocolate, chopped
60 ml/¼ cup coconut oil or
  60 g/¼ cup non-hydrogenated
  sunflower spread
¼ teaspoon salt
110 g/2 cups plain corn flakes,
  with no added sugar

*2 x 12-hole muffin pans, lined with
(eco-friendly) paper cases*

This is one of the most popular if not THE most popular product that I prepare for events and parties. It's so simple, yet it's so addictive and impossible not to like. This is the treat I give to someone if I'm really trying to show them that living healthily while still enjoying indulgent foods from time to time IS possible. In other words, it's a converter.

Put the chocolate, coconut oil and salt in a heatproof bowl over a saucepan of barely simmering water. Leave until melted and completely smooth.

Tip the corn flakes into the melted chocolate. Mix thoroughly with a wooden spoon but don't be afraid to crush some of the corn flakes. Scoop a generous tablespoon of the mixture into each muffin case, patting the mixture down as you go. Put the whole muffin pans in the freezer for 15 minutes.

Remove the cakes from the freezer just before serving. Store them in the freezer for up to 2 weeks.

Did you know?
Sometimes when you want to overhaul your diet, the first steps are the hardest to establish. You swap your cereal for chia seeds, eat big salads and stock your fridge full of healthy snacks. This approach can often be overwhelming and send us straight back to our old ways. Even though it's tempting to go "all in" because you want all the benefits of a heathy lifestyle, you're more likely to have success by doing what I recommend to all my clients – pick 3 small changes you'd like to make each week. This will give you measurable victories and you'll be able to pinpoint the effects of each change more finely. And you'll be intrigued to keep going too!

Chocolate-covered banana fudgesicles

Makes 8

4 large bananas
215 ml/1 cup coconut oil
60 g/½ cup unsweetened
    cocoa powder
3 tablespoons agave syrup
1 tablespoon stevia, or more
    agave syrup

8 wooden skewers
freezer-proof baking sheet or plate,
    lined with clingfilm/plastic wrap

Every Friday after school as a child, my mother would take me and my sister to the local store where we were allowed to pick one treat each. During the winter, we figured it was smarter to go for a bag of candy, which could last us all week if we stuck to eating a few each day. This strategy worked until we discovered the ice-cream cabinet and fell in love with those ice-cream lollies on a stick, covered in chocolate. It goes without saying they lasted us all of 5 minutes.

I think most people I know love chocolate, love bananas and love nuts. When you put all these together, you have a snack made in heaven. Here's how to do ice-cream lollies the healthy way. In principle, fixing yourself one of these involves freezing some banana on a stick and covering it in healthy chocolate, but I've included all the fun variations. This is a great recipe to make with kids or for kids. Just make sure you don't use wooden skewers with sharp ends.

Peel the bananas and cut each one in half through the centre. Trim the pointy ends if you like. Spear each portion onto a skewer and freeze for at least 2 hours. It's useful to keep some peeled bananas in your freezer for everyday use, such as for smoothies, Banana Soft Serve (page 102), or to slice and mix into yogurt – yum!

Put the coconut oil, cocoa powder and agave syrup in a saucepan over medium heat and allow to melt. Stir together, then remove from the heat. Stir in the stevia.

Remove the frozen bananas from the freezer and dip into the melted chocolate mixture. Place onto the prepared baking sheet and freeze immediately until solidified – about 5 minutes.

Variations
Nutty: coat the chocolate-dipped bananas in finely chopped mixed nuts (eg hazelnuts or almonds) or desiccated coconut.
Filled: slice the raw bananas in half lengthways, fill the middle with just under 1 tablespoon of nut butter, then freeze. Coat as before.
Quick pick-me-up: slice the raw bananas in half lengthways, fill the middle with just under 1 tablespoon of nut butter, then freeze. Slice the banana sandwich into 5-cm/2-inch pieces, then coat in the chocolate and finely chopped mixed nuts.

Raw tartlets

Makes 4

145 g/1 cup almonds
135 g/³⁄₄ cup dates, stoned
2 tablespoons unsweetened
   desiccated coconut, or
   more almonds
a pinch of salt
2 teaspoons coconut oil

Mint chocolate filling
   (to fill 2 tarts)
1 large banana
60 ml/¼ cup coconut oil
60 ml/¼ cup pure maple syrup
40 g/⅓ cup unsweetened
   cocoa powder
6 fresh mint leaves or ½ teaspoon
   mint extract

Key lime filling
   (to fill 2 tarts)
½ banana
1 small avocado
60 ml/¼ cup coconut oil
2½ tablespoons pure maple syrup
freshly squeezed juice of 1 lime

4 tartlet moulds

I never used to like tarts, until I tried a raw version in a New York vegan restaurant that I fell in love with. With raw desserts, a mix of nuts and dried fruits are often used to replace pastry, which makes them a lot more soft and chewy, and I think that's what converted me.

The great thing about raw desserts is that you can be a lot looser when preparing them, feeling free to alter as you want; because nothing is baked, there's no need to be as precise with your measurements. Consider this recipe as a guideline – if you want to add some more sweetener, or switch up the mint for orange extract for example, feel free. Though this recipe may look complicated, don't be intimidated – essentially, it's blending 3 rounds of ingredients in the food processor, and using your freezer or fridge to set them.

Put the almonds in a food processor fitted with an "S" blade and blitz until crumbly. Add the dates, desiccated coconut, salt and coconut oil and pulse until a smooth mixture forms. Remove the dough from the processor and divide it into 4. Press each portion into a tartlet mould so that it neatly lines the base and sides of the mould. Ideally you want the tartlet cases to be about 1 cm/½ inch thick all the way around, with plenty of room for the filling. Don't worry if you have a little extra dough – you can roll this into bite-size energy balls and save for a healthy snack later on.

For both the fillings, make sure the coconut oil is liquid. If it isn't, put it in a saucepan over low heat and allow to melt. Allow to cool completely, otherwise the hot oil will start to cook the other ingredients in the filling.

Place each set of filling ingredients in the food processor, one set at a time, and blitz until smooth. Divide each filling between 2 tartlet cases and freeze for at least 15 minutes to set.

Raw tarts will keep, in the freezer, for up to 2 weeks, so they're a great make-ahead option for tea and dinner parties.

Cookies & Bakes

Cut out wheat, and you cut out baking, right? Wrong! Cookies, cakes and even doughnuts can all be enjoyed if you just know how to replace conventional baking ingredients with healthier and widely available alternatives. You can still tuck into a slice of banana cake, serve up a melting chocolate fondant for a dinner party, or wolf down a sticky cinnamon roll for elevenses, all in the knowledge that you aren't going to come crashing down after your initial sugar high. These recipes are designed to answer that need for home-baked yumminess, warm from the oven, that simply can't be forgone, no matter what your dietary choices in life.

Chocolate chip cookies

Makes about 16

125 ml/½ cup almond milk
2 tablespoons ground flaxseeds/
    linseeds
285 g/2 cups spelt flour
75 g/⅔ cup unsweetened
    cocoa powder (preferably raw)
1¼ teaspoons bicarbonate of/
    baking soda
125 ml/½ cup sunflower oil
190 g/1 cup granulated sweetener
    of choice
1 tablespoon vanilla extract
175 g/1 cup dark/bittersweet
    chocolate chips

2 baking sheets lined with foil

I first went vegan in the summer of 2009. I had flirted with the idea before but resisted taking the plunge because I thought it would be too difficult. I decided I'd give it a spin for a month, because that seemed doable enough and I was so curious to see if I would feel any different. Almost immediately I slept so much better at night and my digestion improved immensely, so I decided to keep it up, but told myself that it wasn't a commitment – I could stop doing it any time I wanted. That summer, I was telling Andy, a chef I knew, about my vegan experiment and my ongoing dessert cravings. So he made me THE most amazing chocolate chip cookies which were better than any I had ever tasted. To this day they remain my favourite treat, and this book wouldn't be complete without it. Thank you to Andy for giving me the recipe.

If it hadn't been for these cookies, it's very possible my vegan experiment wouldn't have stuck, because I would have likely resorted to conventional cookies when I had a craving. I owe a lot to this recipe!

Preheat the oven to 180°C (350°F) Gas 4.

Mix together the almond milk and ground flaxseeds/linseeds and set aside to thicken for a few minutes.

Separately, whisk together the flour, cocoa powder and bicarbonate of/baking soda in a large bowl.

Add the sunflower oil, sweetener and vanilla extract to the milk-seed mixture and stir thoroughly. After about 5 minutes you'll start to see it thicken up even more.

Pour the liquid mixture into the bowl of dry ingredients and stir to combine. It will look far too liquidy to resemble regular cookie dough, so set it aside for about 10–15 minutes and you'll see it change. Stir it again once thick.

Pinch off pieces of dough a little smaller than a golf ball and roll into balls between your hands. Flatten them to discs about 1 cm/½ inch thick and arrange on the prepared baking sheets. They will spread a lot during baking, so leave plenty of space between them.

Bake the cookies in the preheated oven for about 7 minutes, after which they will seem too soft to remove, but they will harden as they cool. Gently transfer the cookies to a wire rack to cool completely. They will still be gooey and soft in the middle, which for me is how a perfect cookie should be. Store in an airtight container for up to 4 days.

Chocolate chip coconut cookies

Makes 15–16

130 g/1 cup gluten-free plain/
  all-purpose flour of choice
60 g/¾ cup unsweetened
  desiccated coconut
1 teaspoon baking powder
½ teaspoon bicarbonate of/
  baking soda
½ teaspoon salt
60 ml/¼ cup coconut oil
100 ml/⅓ cup agave syrup
1 teaspoon vanilla extract
85 g/½ cup dark/bittersweet
  chocolate chips

baking sheet lined with foil
heart-shaped cookie cutter (optional)

I created these heart-shaped cookies for a Valentine one year, because we shared a love of coconut water. I set out to craft a coconut-flavoured treat and added the chocolate because, well, that's the flavour of Valentine's Day! Since then, I've made these cookies probably more than I've made any other baked goodie because they are a unanimous crowd pleaser, any day of the year.

Preheat the oven to 180°C (350°F) Gas 4.

Mix the flour, coconut, baking powder, bicarbonate of/baking soda and salt in a large bowl. You may want to sift the baking powder and bicarbonate of/baking soda with the flour first, since it's essential that these are evenly spread throughout your cookie dough before it goes in the oven.

Make sure the coconut oil is liquid. If it isn't, put it in a saucepan over low heat and allow to melt. Allow to cool completely, otherwise the hot oil will start to cook the other ingredients in the filling. Now make sure there's exactly 60 ml/¼ cup; sometimes it can be a little more or less than the initial quantity.

Mix the coconut oil, agave syrup and vanilla extract together. Bear in mind that they won't combine very easily because the oil and agave are very different consistencies, but do your best to give it a good stir.

Pour the wet mixture into the bowl of dry ingredients and mix with a wooden spoon. Add the chocolate chips. With your hands, compress the cookie dough into a ball, making sure the chocolate chips are incorporated.

Take 1 generous tablespoon of cookie dough into your hands at a time, compress it and roll it into a ball. You can either flatten the balls slightly on the prepared baking sheet to make round cookies, or you can press the ball of dough into the cookie cutter to mould it into a heart shape. Don't worry if the dough seems a little oily – this is normal. Bake the cookies in the preheated oven for about 10–12 minutes, until they start to brown slightly. Remove the baking sheet from the oven and, using a spatula, transfer the cookies to a wire rack and allow to cool for at least 5 minutes before serving. Store in an airtight container for up to 3 days.

Fig rolls

Makes 35–40

Crust
90 g/1 cup oats or oat flour
165 g/1½ cups ground almonds/
    almond meal
½ teaspoon salt
1 teaspoon baking powder
60 ml/¼ cup coconut oil
120 ml/½ cup agave syrup
60 ml/¼ cup unsweetened apple
    purée/applesauce
2 teaspoons vanilla extract

Fig filling
150 g/1 cup dried figs, hard stems
    cut off
3 tablespoons freshly squeezed
    lemon juice
1 tablespoon agave syrup
¼ teaspoon ground ginger
1 tablespoon water (optional)

*baking sheet lined with baking
parchment*

As a child, I didn't like much in the candy department that wasn't strawberry flavoured. However, I made an exception for those doughy rolls filled with a sweet fig centre, known as Fig Newtons or fig rolls. Their concept was based on an ancient Egyptian delicacy and popularized by American conglomerate Nabisco, who produced them in the flat cylindrical shape we know today.

Though the recipe may seem long and complicated, it's pretty foolproof, so if you've never baked before this is a great one to start with!

For the crust
If using oats, put them in a food processor and grind to a fine flour. Put the oat flour, ground almonds/almond meal, salt and baking powder in a bowl and mix.

Separately, combine the coconut oil, agave syrup, apple purée/applesauce and vanilla extract. Sift the dry ingredients into the bowl of wet ingredients and mix well. Refrigerate for at least 1 hour.

For the fig filling
Meanwhile, put the figs, lemon juice, agave syrup and ground ginger into the food processor and pulse until a smooth paste forms. If your mixture isn't moving, gradually drizzle in the water as needed.

Once your dough has properly chilled, preheat the oven to 180°C (350°F) Gas 4.

Divide the dough into 4. Take one portion and place it between 2 sheets of baking parchment. Using a rolling pin, roll it out into a rectangle about 25 x 10 cm/10 x 4 inches. Spread one quarter of the fig filling along one long edge of the dough rectangle, leaving a little border around it. Fold the bare half of the rectangle over onto the filling, then seal the ends of the rectangle by pressing the dough together with your fingers.

Repeat this process with the remaining portions of dough and filling. Arrange the dough cylinders on the prepared baking sheet. Bake in the preheated oven for about 12–14 minutes, until the outside is slightly browned. Allow to cool completely, then cut into fat slices. Store in an airtight container for up to 5 days.

Peanut butter and jelly thumbprint cookies

Makes about 12

125 g/1 cup gluten-free plain/
   all-purpose flour of choice
¼ teaspoon salt
¼ teaspoon bicarbonate of/
   baking soda
1 teaspoon baking powder
45 g/¼ cup granulated sweetener
   of choice
60 ml/¼ cup pure maple syrup
1 teaspoon vanilla extract
5 tablespoons peanut butter
1½ tablespoons coconut oil
a few large tablespoons of
   no-added-sugar strawberry jam

*baking sheet lined with baking
   parchment*

If you are a fan of "sweet and salty" in your treats, this recipe is designed with you in mind. I tried making a plain vanilla cookie once, but used nut butter as my fat instead of sunflower spread as I didn't have any to hand. I instantly loved that kiss of salt it gave the cookies, but I felt it could be taken up a notch. Building in a dollop of strawberry jam was the obvious alteration, since that flavour combination is a no-fail, much-loved favourite. I like to think of these as the fancy version of little peanut-butter-and-jelly finger sandwiches, appropriate for even the smartest of tea parties (just make enough for lunchbox leftovers the next day).

Preheat the oven to 180°C (350°F) Gas 4.

Sift together the flour, salt, bicarbonate of/baking soda and baking powder in a bowl. Add the sweetener and stir well.

Separately, combine the maple syrup, vanilla extract, peanut butter and coconut oil. Stir until the peanut butter has liquefied.

Add the wet mixture to the bowl of dry ingredients and incorporate well, but be sure not to overmix.

Pinch off small pieces of dough and roll into balls between your hands. Flatten them slightly between your palms and arrange them on the prepared baking sheet. Using the back of a teaspoon, press a small well in the middle of each cookie. Bake the cookies in the preheated oven for 10 minutes. Remove the baking sheet from the oven and spoon a little dollop of jam into the well in each cookie but don't fill them up to the top, as the jam will rise when heated. Return the baking sheet to the oven and bake for a further 5 minutes.

Remove the cookies from the oven and allow them to cool completely before eating. Store in an airtight container for up to 3 days.

Banana cake

Serves about 14

3 teaspoons ground chia seeds
   (buy them ready ground, or
   grind whole seeds in a coffee/
   spice grinder)
3 tablespoons water
2 very ripe bananas
250 g/1 cup + 1 tablespoon
   non-dairy spread or coconut oil
340 g/2½ cups gluten-free plain/
   all-purpose flour of choice
3⅓ teaspoons baking powder
1 teaspoon salt
225 g/1 cup xylitol
1 teaspoon vanilla extract

22–23-cm/9-inch bundt/ring pan
(the hole in the middle should be
about 10 cm/4 inches wide), or
23-cm/9-inch round cake pan,
greased

When I think about dishes that have played a significant part in the memories I treasure, my grandmother's banana cake always comes to mind first. Growing up, there wasn't a single week in my life that I didn't eat it. We saw her almost every day after school, and she was always in the kitchen making incredible Indian food. Being children, this didn't interest us much, but her super-soft banana cake would entice us the way it did anyone else who ever tasted it. It got to a point where people would beg her to make them a cake once they tried it, from our school friends to the plumbers who came to fix her bathroom.

When I decided to cut dairy and eggs from my diet, banana cake was the first baked good I tried to make a healthy version of. Somehow, it turned out perfectly. If it hadn't, I don't think my venture into healthy baking would have ever turned out to be more than a one-time experiment. Of course, my healthified banana cake won't ever be as good as my grandmother's, because she had that magic touch that all good bakers do, but the recipe was one of the best things she gave me.

Preheat the oven to 160°C (320°F) Gas 3.

Put the ground chia seeds in a small bowl with the water. Whisk the seeds into the water with a fork until the mixture starts to feel like the consistency of a beaten egg – in fact, what you have are 3 "chia eggs" that play the same role as eggs in plant-based baking recipes. Place in the fridge.

Meanwhile, mash the bananas with a fork and set aside.

Put the spread or coconut oil in a saucepan over low heat and leave just until softened.

In a large bowl, sift together the flour, baking powder, salt and xylitol. Add the vanilla extract, chia mixture, and soft spread or coconut oil and stir well. Gently fold in the bananas.

Spoon the mixture into the prepared baking pan and bake in the preheated oven for 40 minutes. Reduce the temperature to 55°C/130°F or the lowest your oven will go. Bake for a further 20 minutes. Cover the cake with foil if it's looking brown on top but it's not baked all the way through yet.

Remove the cake from the oven and allow to cool for 15 minutes before serving. Store in an airtight container for up to 3 days.

Single-serving chocolate cake

Serves 1

1 tablespoon ground flaxseeds/
linseeds
3 tablespoons water
3 tablespoons gluten-free plain/
all-purpose flour
1 tablespoon unsweetened
cocoa powder
1 tablespoon xylitol or stevia
¼ teaspoon baking powder
a pinch of salt (optional)
2 tablespoons almond milk
1 teaspoon nut butter of choice
1½ tablespoons dark/bittersweet
chocolate chips

*1 ceramic mug or large ramekin –
microwave- or oven-safe,
depending on your chosen
baking method*

Sometimes, you want a sweet, chocolatey fix to end your day with but have neither the time nor the energy to go into full baking mode. This recipe makes enough cake for one person, so you're not left with a ton of waste or second helpings to tempt you away from your healthy intentions. There's also minimal clean-up involved, so it's ideal for whipping up just before your favourite TV show's about to start.

I'm not a huge fan of microwaving food in general, but this is one recipe where this method can really come in handy if you so choose. If not, an oven is just fine too – you'll just have to wait a few extra minutes for your cake.

Put the flaxseeds/linseeds and water in a small bowl. Whisk the seeds into the water with a fork until the mixture starts to feel like the consistency of a beaten egg – in fact, what you have is a "flax egg" that plays the same role as an egg in plant-based baking recipes. Place in the fridge.

You can use a microwave or an oven for this recipe. If using an oven, preheat it to 180°C (350°F) Gas 4.

In your chosen mug or ramekin, combine the flour, cocoa powder, sweetener, baking powder and salt, if using. Add the "flax egg", almond milk and nut butter and stir until smooth. Add the chocolate chips – you can either let these sit on top so that they seep into the cake when melted, or you can mix them in so they're evenly distributed throughout the cake.

If using a microwave, microwave the cake on high for about 45–60 seconds, until cooked through. If using an oven, bake for 5–6 minutes – no more than that, because it tastes best when the centre is still slightly gooey.

Did you know?
For a lot of us, the end of the evening is when all our healthy intentions can fall apart. We eat like saints until dinner, have a little dessert and end up beating ourselves up and feeling racked with guilt. I've found the key is to factor random indulgences into your plans, so that when you feel like treating yourself after dinner on occasion, it doesn't feel like failure. You'll be able to enjoy eating the treats even more too.

Sticky carrot bites

Makes about 32

1½ tablespoons ground flaxseeds/
linseeds
4½ tablespoons water
150 g/1¼ cups gluten-free plain/
all-purpose flour of choice
½ teaspoon xanthan gum
2 teaspoons baking powder
1 teaspoon bicarbonate of/
baking soda
¾ teaspoon salt
2 teaspoons ground cinnamon
½ teaspoon ground ginger
½ teaspoon grated nutmeg
(optional) – I usually prefer this
recipe without nutmeg, but
carrot cake purists may want
to add this in
190 g/1 cup xylitol
125 ml/½ cup unsweetened apple
purée/applesauce
60 ml/¼ cup almond milk
125 ml/½ cup olive oil
190 g/1½ cups finely grated carrots
(about 6–8 carrots) – the finer
you can grate these, the better
large handful of raisins (no need
to measure)
large handful of walnuts

23-cm/9-inch square baking pan
baking sheet lined with foil

These gooey little bites are to carrot cake what brownies are to chocolate cake. They are softer and more caramel-like than traditional carrot cake, and definitely less fancy. I have learned from catering tea parties that very often people are more willing to try smaller sizes of treat, because it only takes a few bites of something sweet to satisfy you. It's also more convenient to eat while you're chatting to friends. Although carrot cake was one of the most common requests we received, it used to remain largely untouched when we made it in the traditional triple-layer shape with tons of frosting. I designed these little bites to provide the same flavours, but in a way that's easier to eat. Anyone who has tried these has told me that they prefer the texture of them to that of the normal cake too.

The trick to a really addictive carrot cake flavour is to use olive oil – its savouriness really balances the flavour profile and stops it from being sickly sweet.

Preheat the oven to 180°C (350°F) Gas 4.

Put the flaxseeds/linseeds and water in a small bowl. Whisk the seeds into the water with a fork until the mixture starts to feel like the consistency of a beaten egg – in fact, what you have is a "flax egg" that plays the same role as an egg in plant-based baking recipes. Place in the fridge.

In a large bowl, combine the flour, xanthan gum, baking powder, bicarbonate of/baking soda, salt, cinnamon, ginger and nutmeg, if using.

Separately, mix together the xylitol, apple purée/applesauce, almond milk and olive oil. Stir in the "flax egg". Pour this into the bowl of dry ingredients and stir until smooth. Add the grated carrots and the raisins and give it a gentle stir just to make sure they are well distributed throughout the mixture.

Spoon the mixture into the baking pan – it's a very wet mixture so you don't need to grease your pan. Crumble the walnuts with your hands and scatter them on top so that they sit on the surface of the cake. Bake in the preheated oven for about 30 minutes. Now cover the cake with foil and return it to the oven for a further 10–12 minutes. This will ensure the cake cooks through without allowing the surface to burn.

Remove the cake from the oven – you will see the insides are still gooey. Cut it into little portions (about 5 x 3 cm/2 x 1½ inches), and place the portions on the prepared baking sheet. Put them in the still-warm oven for a further 30 minutes, or less if you prefer them to stay gooey. Store in an airtight container for up to 3 days.

Bread and butter pudding with grilled peaches

Serves 6

4 peaches
6 slices of gluten-free bread
(the crustier, the better!)
2–3 tablespoons coconut oil
or non-hydrogenated sunflower
spread
large handful of raisins and/or
sultanas/golden raisins – I like
a mix of both
500 ml/2 cups coconut milk (try
not to substitute this for another
non-dairy milk, as the thicker
coconut milk stands in for
double/heavy cream here)
3 tablespoons xylitol or stevia
(xylitol will work better here)
1½ tablespoons cornflour/
cornstarch
1 teaspoon ground cinnamon

6 ramekins

When I lived in India, there was an English café I went to almost every afternoon for tea; they served the most delicious bread and butter pudding made with croissant bread. It was to die for! I can't imagine how much butter and cream went into it, and at the time it wasn't a concern of mine, so I happily ate it every day.

This is a cleaned-up version that includes grilled/broiled peaches which work really well here. Most bread and butter puddings are made in large glass baking dishes but I like to make little individual puddings in individual ramekins. This way you can eat straight from the ramekin rather than cut it up and serve it on a plate, which makes it look messy. It's easier to halve the recipe this way, too.

Preheat the grill/broiler to medium.

Stone the peaches, then cut the flesh into cubes. Place them in an ovenproof dish and grill/broil them until they start to caramelize – about 3 minutes.

Remove the peaches from the grill/broiler, and preheat the oven 180°C (350°F) Gas 4.

Toast the slices of bread, then spread the coconut oil or sunflower spread over both sides of each slice. Cut the toast into cubes about 2 cm/1 inch wide. Mix with the peaches and dried fruit, then divide the mixture equally between the ramekins.

Put the coconut milk and sweetener in a saucepan over medium heat and leave until warm. Now stir in the cornflour/cornstarch and you will see the mixture start to thicken up. Remove the pan from the heat and allow the mixture to cool until it is lukewarm. Stir in the cinnamon, then pour the mixture equally into the ramekins.

Bake the puddings in the preheated oven for about 25–30 minutes, until firm. They are best served freshly baked, but they can also be reheated for 4–5 minutes the day after baking.

Cinnamon buns

Makes about 8

Dough

2¼ teaspoons quick yeast (be precise! With yeasted recipes, the teeniest adjustments can make a big difference)
250 ml/1 cup warm (not hot) water
125 ml/½ cup agave syrup or pure maple syrup
360 g/3 cups gluten-free plain/all-purpose flour, plus extra for dusting
1 tablespoon ground cinnamon
1 tablespoon baking powder
1 teaspoon salt
½ teaspoon xanthan gum
175 ml/¾ cup coconut oil
1 teaspoon vanilla extract
2 tablespoons apple cider vinegar

Filling

130 g/1 cup almonds
1 teaspoon ground cinnamon
75 g/½ cup coconut sugar, or other granulated sweetener of choice (coconut sugar gives the buns an earthy, caramel-y taste)
a few large tablespoons non-hydrogenated sunflower spread, for spreading

Glaze

95 g/½ cup xylitol
2–3 tablespoons almond milk

round baking pan or Pyrex dish, 23-cm/9-inch diameter, greased

These are your new go-to bakes for special-occasion tea parties, long, lazy brunches and cosy weekends out of the cold.

For the dough
Put the yeast and warm water in a bowl and mix. Mix in the agave or maple syrup and let sit. You will see foam start to form on the surface – this is good!

Put the flour, cinnamon, baking powder, salt and xanthan gum in a large bowl and mix with a balloon whisk to make sure everything is well incorporated. Mix the coconut oil, vanilla and vinegar into the yeast mixture. Now stir this into the bowl of dry ingredients with a wooden spoon. It will be very sticky and light but that's normal. Cover lightly with clingfilm/plastic wrap, then a damp cloth, and allow to rise for 1 hour.

Uncover the dough and poke it: if it bounces back, it is ready. (If not, rest it a little longer.) Sprinkle flour generously over the dough and form it into a ball. It will be very stretchy, so add as much flour as needed. Freeze for 15 minutes.

For the filling
Blitz the almonds, cinnamon and sugar in a food processor until crumbly.

Preheat the oven to 200°C (400°F) Gas 6.

Dust flour over a large surface and place the dough on top. Knead it well by stretching it away from itself with your palms and squashing it back together. Flour as you go along. Don't be disconcerted if the dough seems elastic and sticky – it will turn out amazingly. Dust more flour on the surface and use a rolling pin to roll out the dough until it's roughly 40 x 25 cm/16 x 10 inches. Warm the sunflower spread between your fingers and spread it over the dough. Scatter the filling over it. Starting from a long edge, roll up the dough very tightly (as it will expand in the oven). Flour the outside of the dough if it's sticking to your surface. Once you have rolled almost all the way, fold the top end over the roll (rather than bringing the roll all the way to the top): this will make it easier to cut. Using a sharp knife, cut the roll into about 10-cm/4-inch slices. Arrange the slices, cut side down, in the prepared dish, leaving a little space between. Bake in the preheated oven for 22–25 minutes, or until a cocktail stick/toothpick inserted in the dough comes out clean.

For the glaze
Blitz the xylitol in a high-speed blender until finely ground. Put in a bowl with 1 tablespoon of the milk. Stir and drizzle in milk until you reach a consistency you like. Remove the buns from the oven, allow to cool for 5 minutes, then drizzle the glaze over them. Store in an airtight container for up to 4 days.

Apple and cinnamon cake

Serves about 14

240 g/2 cups gluten-free plain/
 all-purpose flour of choice
3½ teaspoons baking powder
1 teaspoon ground cinnamon
½ teaspoon salt
475 ml/2 cups unsweetened apple
 purée/applesauce
120 ml/½ cup agave syrup or pure
 maple syrup (maple syrup works
 particularly well here)
80 ml/⅓ cup rice milk
75 g/½ cup sultanas/golden raisins,
 raisins, or a mixture of both (or
 even chocolate chips, but the
 dried fruit goes particularly well
 with the apple-cinnamon flavours)

*22–23-cm/9-inch bundt/ring pan
 (the hole in the middle should be
 about 10 cm/4 inches wide),
 20-cm/8-inch square baking pan,
 or 23-cm/9-inch round cake pan*

If you are new to cake making and particularly to baking with healthy ingredients, this is a great recipe to wet your toes with. It's so easy to put together and there's very little room for error. I first made it last autumn when on the first really cosy Saturday of the season, I (rather shockingly) didn't feel like chocolate in the afternoon. Seeing leaves on the ground and lighting my fire for the first time, I got the idea for this cake based on the flavours we associate with this time of year. Yes, they are clichéd flavours, but who cares when they're this good? I'm not even a huge apple lover but it's impossible to keep me away from this cake.

Preheat the oven 180°C (350°F) Gas 4.

Sift the flour and baking powder together into a bowl, then add the cinnamon and salt and mix by hand. Create a hole or a well in the centre of the ingredients – you will pour the wet mixture into this well later and this method will prevent too much lumpiness in the batter.

Separately, combine the apple purée/applesauce, agave syrup and rice milk. Pour this wet mixture, one third at a time, into the well in your bowl of dry ingredients. Stir as you go, preferably with a spatula but a wooden spoon will be fine too. Be sure not to overmix, and don't worry about a few lumps. Add the dried fruit and make sure it is well distributed throughout the mixture.

Spoon the mixture into the baking pan – it's a very wet mixture so you don't need to grease your pan. Bake in the middle of the preheated oven for 40 minutes, or until a cocktail stick/toothpick inserted into the middle of the cake comes out clean. Cover the cake with foil if it's looking brown on top but it's not baked all the way through yet. Allow the cake to cool for at least 10 minutes before cutting into it. Store in an airtight container for up to 3 days.

Mini baked doughnuts with cinnamon "sugar"

Makes 24

Doughnuts
160 g/1⅓ cups gluten-free plain/
  all-purpose flour
½ teaspoon xanthan gum
65 g/⅓ cup xylitol
1½ teaspoons baking powder
1 teaspoon bicarbonate of/
  baking soda
1 teaspoon ground cinnamon
½ teaspoon salt
125 ml/½ cup almond or rice milk
2 tablespoons apple cider vinegar
1½ tablespoons sunflower oil
5 tablespoons unsweetened apple
  purée/applesauce
1 teaspoon vanilla extract

Cinnamon "sugar"
1 big serving spoon
  non-hydrogenated sunflower
  spread (about 60 ml/¼ cup, but
  it doesn't need to be precise)
2 teaspoons ground cinnamon
5 tablespoons xylitol or stevia

one or two mini-doughnut pans
  (enough to make 24 doughnuts),
  greased with coconut oil or
  sunflower spread
disposable sandwich bag, or piping
  bag fitted with a plain nozzle/tip

A good doughnut can evade even the most accomplished bakers, and I think that's because everyone knows what the perfect one should taste like, so there's very little wiggle room to make a slightly "different" doughnut. It's pretty unanimous that a great doughnut is airy, moist and soft. When baking without a ton of eggs to help us with the fluffiness, it's essential to use both baking powder and bicarbonate of/baking soda to make the batter rise the way we want it to, and xanthan gum for texture. Once you have all your ingredients assembled though, this is one of the easiest baked goods from the book to make, and really fast too. It's a great one to make with kids: for an added bit of fun, you can set up stations of melted chocolate, sprinkles, desiccated coconut and various other toppings so that they can customize their glaze.

For the doughnuts
Preheat the oven to 180°C (350°F) Gas 4.

Put the flour, xanthan gum, xylitol, baking powder, bicarbonate of/baking soda, cinnamon and salt in a large bowl. Stir with a balloon whisk.

Put the milk and vinegar in a small bowl; you will see a kind of "buttermilk" start to form after a couple of minutes. Once this happens, add the sunflower oil, apple purée/applesauce and vanilla extract. Pour the wet mixture into the bowl of dry ingredients and you should see some bubbles form – this is what will make the doughnuts nice and fluffy! Use the whisk again to stir really gently, and stop as soon as the mixtures have combined.

If you have a piping bag, fill the bag with the mixture. If not, fold down your sandwich bag a few times and using a spoon, scoop the mixture into one bottom corner of the bag. Twist the end of the bag to prevent any air from coming in, then use a pair of scissors to snip off the filled corner of the bag – you'll want the cut to be about 1 cm/½ inch long. Pipe the mixture into the holes of the doughnut pan(s). Bake in the preheated oven for 5–6 minutes and keep an eye on them – they are so small that they bake very quickly.

For the cinnamon "sugar"
Melt the sunflower spread and put in a bowl. Separately, combine the cinnamon and sweetener. Remove the baked doughnuts from the pan(s) and dip the top of each one into the melted sunflower spread, then straight into the cinnamon "sugar". Serve immediately – they taste best when straight from the oven, but they will also keep for about 2 days in an airtight container.

Secretive chocolate fondants

Makes 10–12

400-g/14-oz. can of black beans
40 g/4 tablespoons gluten-free flour
  (buckwheat or quinoa work well)
4 tablespoons unsweetened
  cocoa powder
½ teaspoon baking powder
¼ teaspoon salt
90 ml/⅓ cup pure maple syrup
  or agave syrup
2 tablespoons xylitol or other
  granulated sweetener (stevia is
  not advisable in this recipe)
45 ml/¼ cup coconut oil
2 teaspoons vanilla extract
2 teaspoons grated orange zest or
  orange oil (or coffee extract,
  peppermint oil or other
  flavouring of choice)
130 g/¾ cup dark/bittersweet
  chocolate chips, or finely
  chopped dark/bittersweet
  chocolate

10–12 ramekins

I love to read healthy eating blogs; they keep me up to date on the newest food products, inspire me to stay healthy and fit, and provide me with ideas for recipes. I had seen several variations of "black bean brownies" all over the blogosphere but I was always hesitant to try them out. To be honest, they sounded kind of disgusting! The trend ceased to disappear though, so I decided to give them a go. It occurred to me though, that since beans are gooey and moist, their efforts might be best put towards a fondant rather than a brownie. My sister got through almost the entire batch the first time I made these, so I knew I was on to a winner. You will need 10–12 ramekins for this recipe.

Preheat the oven to 180°C (350°F) Gas 4.

Drain the beans well, then put in a food processor and blitz until completely smooth. Add the remaining ingredients, including most of the chocolate chips, and blitz again until everything is well incorporated and the chips aren't visible any more.

Divide the mixture between the ramekins, filling them only two thirds full. You don't need to grease the ramekins before filling them. Scatter the last of the chocolate chips on top.

Bake in the preheated oven for about 15 minutes. Allow to cool for 5 minutes before digging right in – they should be really gooey and soft on the inside. They are best served immediately, but will keep for 5–6 hours at room temperature. You can also keep them refrigerated for 2–3 days and heat them for 5 minutes as needed.

Index

Acknowledgments

After being an avid cookbook reader for many years, being on the other side of the process has made me realize what a collaborative effort it is. Though there may be technically one author, there are so many talents that come together to bring the ideas to life. Thank you Julia, Lucy, Clare, Céline, Leslie, Lauren and everyone else involved at Ryland Peters & Small for lending all your amazing talents. I learned so much from you. Every day that I got to work with you brought me so much excitement and anticipation. Thank you to Cindy in particular for believing I could write a cookbook before I even knew I could, and making the magic happen from the top down.

Tamara Mellon, thank you for being the shining example of how much a woman can achieve in the world while never compromising on who she is, or changing herself for others. Words can't describe how grateful I am to you. Everything I know about being a woman with entrepreneurial aspirations came from the years spent under your wing. I hope to be just like you when I grow up.

Thank you to Char Pilcher and Jane Hamilton, kindred spirits I will always treasure and support. I couldn't do without the ears you lend me.

Thank you to Calgary Avansino, who has supported me from Day One: you truly are my fairy godmother and I feel very blessed to have got to know you.

Thank you to Sarah Stacey, Alex Steinherr, Kayla Jacobs, Eve Kalinik and all the other amazing girls who have been so supportive and wonderful with Upcakes. I am so grateful for your help.

Thank you Sanj, Raj and the whole of Dephna Group. Thank you Kara Rosen and all of your wonderful team.

Thank you Maui, Josie, Edwin and Agnes for all your help with this book and with my day-to-day business.

Thank you James Rae for the ever-interesting conversation and for effortlessly spreading your magic everywhere you go.

Thank you to all the people I feel lucky to call friends, family and adopted family.

Thank you PJ for always being my number one and supporting me as much as you do.

Thank you David and Freddie for setting the best example of ambition and hard work that anyone could ever wish for.

Thank you Amelia, Sarah and Cleo for all the inspiration you constantly give me.

Thank you Beebs for always making me laugh and sharing my views on the world. Just being around you is a joy.

To Sofia, life wouldn't be it without you. Nothing is official until we have had a check-in.

Papa, knowing that I have a soul twin in this world gives me permission to be truly me. Thank you for being patient, open-minded, selfless and dogged in your teaching. Mama, thank you for giving every ounce of yourself to me and then some. Thank you for being all the good things I am not. I will cherish our mother-daughter bond in many lifetimes to come.